UPON THIS ROCK

By The Mission

A NEW CATHOLIC CATECHISM

UPON THIS ROCK

The Story of the Mission Singers

Brother Jack Coyne and
Brother Donald Middendorf

Exposition Press　　　*New York*

EXPOSITION PRESS INC.

50 Jericho Turnpike   Jericho, New York 11753

FIRST EDITION

© 1970 by Jack Coyne and Donald Middendorf. *All rights reserved, including the right of reproduction in whole or in part in any form except for short quotations in critical essays and reviews.* Manufactured in the United States of America.

LIBRARY OF CONGRESS CATALOG CARD NUMBER: 70-130405

To

Father Joachim Lally, O.S.B.,

a friend forever of the Mission

UPON THIS ROCK

Foreword

"Religion," says The Mission, "is life. When four or five kids, each from disadvantaged homes and splintered backgrounds, reach out to you and plead for a future, there isn't any doubt in your mind. You must say yes. This 'yes' is what religion is all about for all of us."

A sensitivity toward the real life around us is one of the major reasons The Mission handles itself so successfully, whether on the concert trail or in the deprived neighborhoods they call home. Although not yet ordained priests, these young men combine their serious seminary training and study with still another professional career. The Mission projects a picture of young men living up to their reputation as one of the finest singing groups in the nation.

In its relatively short singing career this young group "has played the Catholic circuit, parish halls, high schools, and coffee houses, shaping their own songs into a polished repertoire. They rub the sights and sounds of slum life into a sensitive expression of human hope." They have appeared on national television and radio, delighting millions on well-known, highly-rated shows.

But there is the other side of The Mission—the young, enthusiastic, humble side, that enables them to be as effective in other areas of life as they are on stage or in a recording studio.

The Mission consists of four young priests-to-be, all studying religiously at St. Louis Divinity School in St. Louis, Missouri. They come from Massachusetts, New York, and Connecticut.

There is nothing typical about any of these men. They have an aware, wide-open attitude that promises an original and straightforward approach towards any of life's problems.

When any one of The Mission speaks with you, you know immediately that this is a group of intelligent, sincere young men, well-rounded in learning and experience, who have learned to mirror both warmth and compassion.

The Mission understands and likes people. They answer questions in a clear, direct, simple manner. They show a genuine sensitivity tempered to the feelings of others.

In their everyday life, communication for The Mission means communication of reality. They try through their songs to describe life as it is.

Life to them is an awareness of human dignity. As they put it,

> We live in an area of desperate need. Christ will always be our inspiration; it is the Christ found in man that we seek. All our efforts, skills and sacrifices, all the material and professional success in the world could not be enough for us if we did not make Christ come alive to our times. For us, religion is trying to do what Christ did when he walked this earth, what he would do if he walked here today: he would see, and conquer poverty, disease, ignorance, and apathy. This is what we try to do. Because we can't do it all alone, we go about the countryside, trying to rally others to the cause of true brotherhood and kindness.

Of these burning realities, The Mission is constantly aware. They have chosen to battle against those things which deprive their less fortunate brothers of happiness and peace on earth. They are devoting their lives to change and betterment, in life. Such dedication to the cause of mankind is always inspiring and thought-provoking, especially in these tumultuous and insecure times.

The story of The Mission is one that persons of different ages and different religious beliefs will find interesting and challenging. If these young men do nothing else but make our tomorrows more optimistic, we will owe them much.

But they do even more. They depict in their lives and in their musical, professional careers an approach to religion, fundamental in its grasp of Christ's message, yet fresh enough in its expression to be exciting as well as effective.

I have known The Mission for some time now. I have observed them closely while they were at work in their neighborhoods, and also have analyzed their musical performances at first hand. They are most surely a credit to their profession of communication through music. I am happy to call The Mission my friends and co-workers. Their story is well worth your attention.

—RON ELZ
Director, National Broadcasting Institute
St. Louis, Missouri

It was Holy Week, 1967. We were seniors at St. Louis University, but we also had behind us three-and-a-half years as amateur folk singers plus an LP album, financed with our own money and bearing our own label: Glasgow, named for a street we once lived on; the studio was Universal Recording Studios in Chicago.

We might have thought we were pretty important, but right at that moment we were tired. We were waiting all alone, with our guitars piled around us, in the lobby of bustling Kennedy Airport in New York. Just looking around and observing the endless flow of humanity, we knew what a long, rough road we'd have to travel before we could ever really take our places as an accepted influence on this frenzied, lovable world.

Peter, Paul, and Mary; The Brothers Four; The Beatles— these were just a handful of the greats we dared hope to compete with. It was a sobering thought. But for all its loneliness and apprehension, this was one of the most exciting moments of our lives. Father Patrick Berkery, our spiritual advisor and friend, had worked a few minor miracles to get four starry-eyed young seminarians from St. Louis to this moment. We were lucky to be here in New York.

Our stay in New York was to last a week, and we looked forward to meeting the people we had idolized at a distance for so many years. We didn't know what to expect, but we knew it was going to be work, work, and more work. As far as we were concerned, that was the only thing in the world worth talking about. Father Berkery made it quite clear that walking the sidewalks of New York and pounding on office doors was the only sure-fire way to get that "lucky break."

New York is not one of the garden spots of America, yet for us, as we traveled towards Leo House, an inexpensive residence run by German nuns on 23rd Street, we were very impressed by New York's man-made majesty. We saw New York as a symbol of man's greatness and power—his ability to influence and achieve, despite complex difficulties. New York definitely had an inspiring effect on us and when we strolled through Times Square that night, mixing with tourists and residents, all colored grotesquely by powerful neon lights and dwarfed by the massive, giant buildings, we somehow knew that we were entering into one of the greatest experiences of our lives. We had an inkling of what it would be and yet when it happened, it was completely unexpected.

Our first stop the next day was at Columbia Record Company and that's when an undreamed chain of events began. . .

Singing, playing the guitar, and music in general were the most important parts of our lives, through our three-and-a-half years of college. When we went out on a concert, when people liked us and applauded, when we saw our names and pictures and stories in the newspapers, this was great! But there had to be more.

Religion was most meaningful and important to us. Couldn't religion *and* music be acceptable as one? We had had varied experiences in both religion and music throughout our lives.

In the minor seminary, every morning before breakfast, we had attended Mass, sung hymns, and asked God's help and guidance for the coming day. In the evenings, we had closed our day with a hymn, especially on some special feast day. In addition to such constant, regular awareness of God in our everyday lives, we had also attended frequent church services, praying and reading the Scriptures. Most of us did not smoke or drink and we had been trained from early youth to clean language. In short, the minor seminary— the traditional seminary high school—found us showing all the outward signs of a Christian.

We were more aware of Christ in our lives than many boys our own age—but something seemed missing. Our faith was routine; it wasn't electrical or vital. We thought of it as being something choked off deep down inside us.

One of the problems of our younger days was that all of us as seminarians had been trained in our own little ghettos, living an isolated and artificial life in some pretty country-side. We felt that, although we planned to be priests one day, we were treated at the seminary like little kids. We couldn't even go off the property or visit town without per-mission. One of us was almost expelled from the seminary for slipping into a nearby Howard Johnson's and buying their famous strawberry shortcake.

This type of personal restriction is inhibiting and unreal to most men. But it wasn't so much that young people were forced to accept this training or the fact that any of us in-dividually rebelled. Rather, we felt this pattern of training was wrong in order to achieve its goal. We couldn't see how such preparation programs could produce effective priests for the future.

We believed that Christianity is more than laws and ceremonies. We were aware that many other young men outside the seminary were doing things we were not and were, perhaps, closer to Christ than we were.

This constant doubt and questioning of fundamental at-titudes and values in our training program made us dis-satisfied with traditional formal expressions of religion, and unhappy with what we considered the insularism of our high-school seminary. We never wanted to stop preparing

to be priests, but we felt a deep need to know we were
training realistically to help others.

We were confused by traditional but apparently out-
dated procedures, for we saw people leaving their faith,
seminaries being reduced, and even some priests and nuns
leaving their posts. We saw confusion and hesitation among
many adults as they tried to cope with the freedoms Vatican
II had made their right. We felt a need to explore new
dimensions of our religion; we wanted to be architects of a
new awakening.

These were some of the reasons we were so pleased when
Father Berkery moved our college seminary to the heart of
the deprived areas in St. Louis and let us enroll at St. Louis
University as regular college students. For these reasons, too,
we supported his vision in allowing the seminarians to move
into apartments within the inner-city. We were gratified,
too, at his constant support and encouragement of our folk-
singing career throughout the years.

Our thoughts about God and our own roles as seminarians
were troubled and a bit shaken by all that had happened in
our own lives and within our Church. One thing we knew
was that our picture of what our Church actually is, was in
sharp contrast to what we thought it should be. But could
we convince people, both in and out of our Church, that
what we were trying to be, and what we wanted to do, was
not only valid but necessary?

We believed that in order for us to become an accepted
force in our Church, we had to first become successful professionally. All we stood for, all we wanted to get involved
in, was new, different, without counterpart. There were no
precedents, so few people really wanted to take the risk.

These were some of our thoughts as we waited outside
Bill Gallagher's plush office in New York. Bill was the all-

time great at Columbia Records until he resigned in 1968. But right now, Bill had the answer we wanted badly.

One consideration of our trip to New York that had not really registered with us was that most of the people we were going to audition before would probably not take us seriously nor professionally. Our interest in coming to New York, of course, lay along other lines than just the commercial. We recognized the power of music over men and we thought that the Church had to get involved there. But what we heard that week was certainly not what we expected or wanted.

Bill Gallagher said it first; but he really said it for everyone else we would meet that week. Bill listened to our album, liked what he heard, but he couldn't give us a contract. He told us quite frankly that his company had once signed up another group of singing seminarians. Their album had also been great, although their music style was more traditional than ours. Bill told us he really preferred our album to theirs; but the fact remained that their album had not moved. Eventually it had to be taken out of the catalogue. "The Church," Bill said, "is just not commercial."

We told Bill that our group was not ordinary, that our music was not chancel choir bits, and not even nice, quiet, restful Gregorian chant. It was everyday, down-to-earth stuff. Bill then talked about a sister in Belgium, who later became the Singing Nun. He asked us what would happen if we did sign a contract. Would we end up by throwing over our religious careers for the limelight of show business? Bill felt, for many reasons, a religious group could never be successful.

We were caught in a bind. We were not choir boys; but then again, we were not about to model ourselves after the Singing Nun, singing up-lift songs with a fast beat. Our music was our own. We wrote the words, worked hard on the music, and our songs came out telling about things we had seen and heard; maybe not very pretty things—civil rights, war, hunger, poverty, and injustice.

Bill spoke to us about the Church and what his religion meant to him as a person. After a while, we saw we were fighting a losing battle. He was not about to give us the chance we needed. We were even a little dismayed by the emphasis he placed upon the traditional kind of religion, as though this was all that Christ was about.

During the week, we visited a great many other powerful executives, some of the most successful men in the world. They all seemed to have the same message: ". . . boys, you're really great, but you'll just never sell records. People today are not ready for you and your musical approach to religion."

We walked the streets and climbed stairs. We visited trade journals, the bibles and handbooks of the record industry. We stopped in at the television stations, carrying our guitars and our music with us. People in the streets used to stop and smile at us. We made quite a sight in our black shirts and Roman collars, piling out of the subways, always lugging our guitars. One priest stopped us and told us curtly to go home and get dressed but another cheered us on, not even noticing our short-sleeved black shirts.

Many of the people we visited were less direct and more subtle than Bill Gallagher had been, but there was no mistaking their firmness. They were all great successes in their fields, yet the most important thing to them—and they never let us forget—was that, even though we were good as an act, we still were stamped with a great big "No Sale." They just couldn't take the chance.

We even visited Monsignor O'Meara, the head of the Propagation of the Faith in the United States, whose offices are in New York. He knew of us because he had once been Rector of the St. Louis Cathedral. He told us he couldn't help us, even if he wanted to; that if he knew the kind of people we wanted to meet, he couldn't give out the information to us. We asked if he could launch us by using us as a spokesman for the poor; we offered to let him use some of our songs.

We were particularly impressed by the friendliness, sympathy, and genuine concern shown us by people of the Jewish faith. These men, especially, went out of their way to help us, because they believed in what we were trying to do. We are particularly indebted to men like Irv Lichtman of *Cashbox*, Mike Gross of *Billboard*, and our very special friend, Herm Schoenfield of *Variety*.

They gave us leads and the names of the right people to visit in the various offices in New York. "Use my name," they would cheerfully say. Irv and Herm set up appointments for us with Vanguard, RCA, Atlantic, and Warner Brothers, to mention but a few record companies. These men wrote about us in their trade journals, and spoke warmly to their friends about "these guys from St. Louis who live in the slums and sing folk songs."

After we had been in New York a few days, it became very apparent that we were not going to get a record contract right away. So we thought that we might speed up the process by snatching a guest spot on nation-wide TV. So we went hiking off to the halls of the three major networks. We met a good friend in Don Mercer, vice-president of NBC. He set up interviews and auditions for the Tonight Show, the Today Show, and a host of others. Robert Dale Martin helped us a great deal. Through him, we met Chalmers Dale of Look Up and Live, a religious program on CBS. Chum later came out to St. Louis and produced two complete shows on our work. Everywhere we told our story and detailed our hopes. We spelled out what we were actually doing, how we were pioneering, combining seminary training with swinging guitars.

The people in the television field were much more open to us than were those in the recording industry. But we learned that, as with everything else, one must have time. Also, at the time, we were not members of any of the requisite unions. So people who wanted to help us, really couldn't; at least not right away. "We'll get in touch with you," many said. "Perhaps we can set something up when you come back to New York. You *are* coming back, aren't you?"

As we sat in different waiting rooms, we became more and more conscious of the seemingly impossible task before us. We had time to reflect on the yards of advice we had received. We were aware of our inadequacies. But we were also young men who knew our own minds, and who were not going to take no for an answer.

Musically, we were self-conscious. But then, we were willing to work. We knew that a successful commercial album is not the result of any one given factor but rather is a combination of talent and hard work. We knew we had a gimmick, with our youth and our collars. But we wanted first to be accepted as above average singers. Only then could our message be carried through the nation and through the churches. Professional know-how and an appealing sound were quite important among our total goals.

Towards the end of the week, we found ourselves in a little, crowded office on West 44th Street, adjacent to the old St. James Theatre. Bob Shanks, producer of the Merv Griffin Show, agreed to audition us. We had previously been over to see his boss at Westinghouse Productions, and he had called Bob, asking him for his opinion. We played our songs and sang with all our hearts, and the whole outside office, including the switchboard operator, broke into applause. Bob liked us—and he liked what we stood for. He said he would help.

Merv Griffin happened to be taping two shows that day. Bob would try to squeeze us in one of them. One of us dropped down to the set and visited with Merv during the rehearsal, just to make sure. Merv had already heard. We were definitely on the first show. Just let Bob work out the details.

We did the first show, right after Rocky Graziano. In fact, Merv later told us that he had to cut Rocky short in order to get us in. People seemed to like what they heard from us that night. The applause was spontaneous and music in our ears. Merv left his desk to come over and speak with us. We got a chance to hint at what we were all about. The whole experience was great for us. We had finally done it— nationwide television. It made us that much more confident.

That night, on the plane back to St. Louis, we didn't say much. We did some serious soul-searching and just stared ahead quietly. We had no record contract, but we had met several good, influential people. A whole new world opened up for us. We at least knew that we were on the right track.

After all, we were not seeking fame and fortune. Nor were we out to become purely commercial acts. We had accomplished more than we set out to do. And we were the wiser for it.

We prayed to God to give us the strength to keep our heads above the temptations; to set aside the fears and the doubts, the grimness of it all. We knew we had entered upon a new world but that we were also part of another new world, meaning that we were "new church." We wanted desperately to maintain a balance in our studies and in our communication apostolate. We needed strength and courage to honor and serve Christ in our brothers.

The week in New York brought a total rededication for all of us. It was an intense experience. We had found a new dimension. We would continue trying—for we had not failed—and in the darkness of that huge 707, we all knew it.

When we returned to our home in St. Louis, we thought as new men. We had renewed faith in ourselves and in our mission. We felt we could change both the hard, commercial world and could also contribute to the Church. The many seeds that had been planted earlier in our lives began to bear fruits.

Our dream was our goal. But now we knew there were many people who believed in us, and who counted on us. Our trip to New York gave us new inspiration and opened up new avenues. We knew we wouldn't always win, but we would present our best. We became a group even closer than before. We had a common, shared goal. The time was not too far away when we would be able to get a record contract, we thought, and then we would have a platform from which to influence both the entertainment world and our Church. Never again would we be afraid; we were acceptable.

Later in St. Louis, we found out how right we were. Letters started to pour in from the Merv Griffin appearance, short though it had been. Requests for concerts tripled in and around the St. Louis area. Four young priests-to-be, who lived and worked among the disadvantaged, who saw the world as sacred, had started to make some noise. People were starting to listen, to notice. And many began to like what they were hearing.

Two

Before 1965, none of us was involved in any kind of serious folk singing. Until then, our musical interests and activities were strictly limited to the regular Church types. At that time, guitars were frowned upon in any setting for a church service.

We feel more strongly about music now. We think it is good for all people, young and old. Whether playing an instrument, or singing, or both, whether informally or formally in a group, music can be something wonderful. Folk music is unsophisticated and sheer fun. You get the chance to pick your own instrument, and you can even select the chords and positions you enjoy the most and are more natural with.

Anyone who enters the musical field, whether for fun or to make a livelihood, can develop a genuine love for it. One thing is sure; music is really a universal idiom.

Many argue that it is necessary to join some specific performing group early in life but this is not always so. Pressures of organized public appearances can sometimes do more harm than good. Performing isn't fun when you hit a wrong note before a huge crowd or let your group down when they need you. Young people especially feel this.

Pressure situations can lessen one's love even for music. We found this out when we had to rehearse regularly for the weekly Sunday mass in the high-school seminary. We had no special motivation, and we were required to appear— same time, same place. Probably as a result, we never cared much for Gregorian chant; practicing became a chore, music class was a drag, singing in church was never any fun. Like anything else, if not handled correctly, music can become distasteful.

Our real interest in folk music developed during our novitiate when the four of us spent an entire year together in a time of spiritual training, and where the ideals of the priesthood were unfolded for us. Of course, all of us had always been zealous devotees of "worldly music." As kids, we had had our own record players and transistor radios. But it wasn't until that year of our novitiate that we saw the possibility of "worldly music" as a valid means of Christian communication.

In those novitiate days, we spent a lot of time listening to Bob Dylan and meditating on the rich, down-to-earth wisdom he offers in his songs. Anyone who came to the castle-like building that was our monastery wondered what we novices found in the seemingly raucous sound of Dylan.

Father Dilgen, our assistant director, tried his utmost to steer us away from Dylan and more towards what he called "valid music." For Father Dilgen, as for many priests at that time, our novitiate year was comparable to a "shining spot" in our lives. Our superiors wanted to keep us away from dirt and pain during that year, to prepare us and to train us for leadership. To us this was a contradiction; we did not believe we could be equipped to work with dirt and pain by isolating us from it.

Once three or four nuns came to the novitiate from town. We don't know what their feelings were at dinner, listening to our kind of music. They loved music, but "valid music." After dinner, we played it again, and the sisters really listened closely to the message songs. They seemed to leave quite changed in their attitude toward "our" music. In fact, later they even called us up and borrowed our records.

Our entire life was deeply imbedded in the Church; all

our friends and memories of younger days were limited completely to religion as rubric and rite—bell, book, and candle. But we wanted to be priests and members of a religious family. This is why our novitiate year occasioned a real crisis for us. Our two loves seemed incompatible: meaningful music and religion. It is true that through religion our lives were filled with music, but it was music, that, for us, seemed deadening and unreal.

We remember during that crucial year discovering people who enjoyed their religion, and who, at the same time, were able to find music that expressed their lives and their love of God. In the area around the novitiate, there were a lot of fundamentalist, Bible-preaching groups. A few times, we visited a camp meeting and found good music, good preaching, and wooden floors with sawdust. Religion was fun for these people, yet at the same time, it meant something. The religious services were very different from the Catholic service we knew, with its staid Latin hymns, and often badly-sung medieval musical selections.

But here, around our novitiate, we saw tents and trailers, whole families camping out on meeting grounds for a week or more, just to attend a religious revival. The minister started the day at breakfast and went right through to supper. Then the really important sessions started in the evening. Everybody seemed to thoroughly enjoy every minute; they seemed to enjoy their religion in an unusual and wonderful way.

Our days in the novitiate were fulfilling. The days were restful, we lived in the country with plenty of wholesome fresh air, good food, and some great experiences. We saw new places and we were a part of the great happiness and family-style living which was so characteristic of seminaries. In many ways, we will always look back on those days with nostalgia, and we remember them with warmth.

Our major interest in music evolved while we were in the novitiate. Although this interest began in conflict, we wanted to prove that contemporary musical forms were not only valid, but also were capable of expressing in an attractive way, really Christian teachings. Towards the latter part of that year, our efforts started to pay off. We could see real results. We faced the difficult task of securing a proficiency and skill in music and, at the same time, beginning to prove our basic thesis by coming up with meaningful examples and material.

This meant hours of hard practice and reflection. We were realistic pioneers, and this is always demanding. Little of the available church music had any basic appeal to us. We considered the rhythms old-fashioned and much too traditional.

Our novice master, Father Werner, encouraged us, but only to a degree. He really never understood what our ideas were all about, although he pretended he did. He couldn't chart a path for us, because we ourselves didn't know where our conflicts would lead us. He did set up opportunities for us to test our ideas, although he considered this permissiveness as letting the "kids do their thing," and if it was successful, he was happy.

Father Werner wanted to help and he tried in his own way. If he had followed his real beliefs, our novitiate year would have been less a search for new musical forms and more a copy of his own "happiest year" as a novice, around 1950.

Our superiors were our friends, yet we felt all alone. We felt these priests could not help us. We had an idea, a conviction, a belief: we had to be on our own. We believed that music and religion could meet in a meaningful way but we were not satisfied with the examples of this combination that were offered us.

We fully realized that if we were going to bring about any significant change in this area, we would have to do it ourselves. This meant creating our own material and putting in hours of study and practice, as a substitute for professional training.

But we felt it had to be done, so we did it. Every chance we got, we rehearsed and sang. If we added up all the time we spent on our music that year, it would probably amount to hundreds of hours. We worked at our music every chance we had.

In the end, it paid off. Those hours of demanding practice made a tremendous contribution to our musical professionalism. We developed a great closeness to one another, and in a sense, we began to come of age, musically. We developed a sense of new direction. No matter what happens to us on the concert stage or off, our close friendship and our music will always be a treasure.

Another important factor that contributed greatly to our early development was the simple and obvious habit of listening over and over again to the albums of Peter, Paul, and Mary. This was a group that was stronger, faster and more professional than we were. Their style was effective and their lyrics really moved their listeners. Their message centered on issues that religions sometimes ignored, such as civil rights, freedom, poverty, individualism.

Peter, Paul, and Mary were everything that we wanted to be. We spent all our days stretching ourselves to be as good or better than others, who like ourselves, had had little formal musical training, but by hard work had "made it" and were getting through to our generation.

Later, many people were impressed by our style and our sound. Many seminarians and nuns were going about playing guitars, but our group always stood out. Our sound was contemporary—our music was down to earth and gripping.

Since every chance we got we practiced our music, at first our studies showed signs of neglect. We did not have regular, organized courses during our novitiate year, for Canon Law did not allow this. But we were supposed to attend a series of lectures regularly.

We were creatures of our times. In Vietnam was what we considered senseless war; President Kennedy had been assassinated; Negroes were beginning to become articulate; our own Church was in ferment. But the issues thrown to us at the lecture table were such things as the meaning of the Midrash interpretation and degrees of human perfection. It all seemed out of touch.

We knew, though, how important are good study habits and school grades to anyone thinking seriously of any career, either in or out of the priesthood. We felt that we could not be an effective instrument of change unless we excelled in our chosen profession. And so we were faced with the double responsibility of trying to develop a meaningful vehicle of religious communication at the same time that we prepared for our principal interest, the priesthood.

We had our problems, as do all seminarians. But, in addition, we believed we were constantly being observed and watched by our superiors, even more than usual, for we were different from many novices. Most ordinary seminary students show less eagerness to question and to experiment than did we. Our attitudes, openly expressed, seemed contrary to the existing novitiate system. It seemed to us as if the superiors were afraid to let us have the freedom we felt necessary to create a different kind of novitiate training.

Our superiors were permissive to a degree but they did not give us total trust. Their seeming reluctance to support us hurt, as can be understood. We were all nineteen or older and like all maturing young people, we did not like to feel we were being treated as children nor having to conform to expected practices. We resented what we considered paternalism from our superiors.

But we realized that half a loaf was better than none. Our concern had always been music, religion, and effective communication. We may have been actually less militant and less revolutionary than we might have been if we had understood the change taking place within us. We could forget the watchful, though paternal, eyes of our superiors when we thought of the importance of what we were trying to do. It was a strange situation; but it was probably a necessary stage in our maturation.

In the eyes of our superiors, music was just a hobby for us; we couldn't disagree with them more vehemently. Music was fast becoming our main goal in life. We worked hard at perfecting ourselves, forging ahead each day. What had started out as a hobby had made us real students of music, forcing us to delve ever more deeply into its reservoirs of feeling. We had put music on a high priority but we strived also to achieve consistently in our regular studies for the priesthood as well.

Despite our problems during the novitiate year, we were able to develop in folk music a serious sensitivity toward style and precise performance. Years later, when we did achieve professional status, we were privileged to meet some of the persons who had provided most of our inspiration that year. By that time, we believed we knew as much about them as they knew about themselves.

When we were recording our first album in New York, we actually sang with Mary Travers, one of the pros whose records and songs had become so much a part of our daily life. As we worked with her in the studio, and talked and laughed together, we had that strange feeling we had gone through all this before.

People always ask us if we ever got into any real trouble

during our seminary days. Although we were a bit *avant-garde,* we never sought confrontation for confrontation's sake. In the high school seminary, we were caught at the usual boyish pranks, like stealing cookies, smoking, talking during silence periods and so on. But nothing serious.

Frankly, in our novitiate, we didn't have time to get into trouble. We were much too busy with prayers, studies, and perfecting our style of music to think of other ways to use up our energies.

Our last few months of that first year found us involved in social work, although the Church never really encouraged such participation for its novices.

Involvement in the problems of others less fortunate than ourselves helped us grow and mature. It helped us become even more determined to tell in music the story of the terrible injustices and indignities some of our fellow men were subjected to—to "tell it like it is."

We wrote words to old tunes again and again, and we even taught the kids we met how to play the guitar. The kids loved to sing along with us, once we taught them the words. Fortunately, they also desperately wanted to play the guitar. Music is so much a universal language and provides so much opportunity for self-expression and personal development, that we found it works wonders in getting through to young people of all classes. Right now, in St. Louis, we manage and help direct three young groups: two are "soul singers," the other is a rock' n' roll group.

We didn't find too many answers to our own questions during our novitiate but each of us made a beginning. What is the Church for? What can music do to reach people? What do young people want? How can we best prepare ourselves for our role in the Church and in the world? Because we were concerned with questions such as these, we knew we were at least able to start to look for answers.

This was brought home to us at a massive rally of nuns, priests, and young people that we attended in the latter part of the year. We were asked to appear as guest performers for this out-of-town convention. There must have been thousands of people there. And we came, in our black robes, guitars swung over our shoulders—an unusual image of the seminarian for that time.

We went on stage and our routines came through smoothly. These were the same routines that we had worked over and over that year. We put all we had into each song we did, and after each the applause became stronger and more enthusiastic. We knew we were accepted. A standing ovation greeted us after the last number; we gave three encores before we left the stage. It appeared we were on the right track.

After the concert, people milled about us. Some were quiet in their comments, others enthusiastic. Everyone seemed to say the same thing: "Thanks for bringing us the message." We were especially gratified by the large numbers of young people who told us they really "dug" our kind of musical approach to religion.

The succeeding days brought our first fan mail. A nun who had been going to quit the convent, because she saw no future for her, wrote us that she might stay. Kids asked us to come to their parish to perform. Priests told us our music was great, to stick to it, even if the going got rough.

We were nearing the end of our first year together, and so much that was exciting and wonderful had happened. No longer did we feel alone; no longer were we unsure. A major hurdle had been passed. Our superiors smiled and took the credit. We were "their boys." But we knew in our hearts the road was still long and arduous. We wondered then who would be there tomorrow to help us.

Music was now our life; we were committed to it; there

was no backing away now. We also were committed to develop music as a means to reach people with the message of true Christianity—and we desperately wanted to be priests. Our Church was changing in theory, but was it really changing in practice? Could we really survive at all? Being a pioneer can be glamorous. But sometimes it can become also dangerous and devastating.

Three

We finished our novitiate in August, 1964 and began our college careers in a small private college in southern Missouri, staffed by the Vincentian Fathers. Our superiors felt that this move offered us the best opportunity possible to further our academic and religious studies.

We probably always had something of the pioneer in us; most of us do. When we packed our belongings, we had no idea of what our new life would be like. Since we had taken our vow of poverty a few days before, we had no money, or individual ownership of material things. But, also, the order was responsible for taking care of our needs.

One thing we had plenty of was good spirits and faith. We all had some misgivings about leaving the area which had been home during our novitiate, because we had made many friends and had achieved so much there. We were a bit disappointed that we would have to spend four years in a small college staffed by priests of a different order; we would have preferred to study with those of our own. But we understood the importance of this move. It meant that the seminary system was opening up, beginning to extend its preparation; we would have a variety of expert teachers and we would experience a more sophisticated scholastic atmosphere. We were determined to do our share to help make our new life in this new region run as smoothly as possible.

We spoke before of the poverty we had freely chosen. But we do not want to leave the impression that we lived a deprived existence. Not at all. We had little or no money in our pockets but we never lacked for good food and suitable clothing. Our order was a good provider and saw that we had all the material things we needed. But at the same time, it never compromised the really important matter of letting us be free of care and worry. That was part of the purpose behind the vow of poverty we had taken—to let us be free to pursue our studies and our apostolates.

We did not fully subscribe to this interpretation of the vow of poverty. We felt that it sometimes made one insensitive to the value of money, while at the same time putting one on a standard of living higher than that enjoyed by many others. One did without a lot of frivolous things, it is true, but one never was given the responsibility of earning his own way, which is important in the development of a mature person.

But we did not let our attitude prevent us from trying to help our order as best we could. We noticed that the tuitions at the college to which we were going would cost more than anticipated, so we tried to be programmed for concerts in and around the area to help out financially. At the same time, we felt we were pulling at least part of our own weight.

All in all, our short stay in southern Missouri worked out very well. Our residence was on top of a hill, in an old mansion that dated back to the Civil War. The town's population numbered about 650, all very delightful, warm people. We met most of them at a parish social where we took our turn with local celebrities, entertaining the crowds. We used to commute to the seminary each morning in a big yellow school bus that someone had donated. At 7:30 every morning, we piled sleepily into the yellow monster and jogged the necessary twelve miles.

We were relieved to be only day students at this seminary. The priests in charge were quite conservative and we could see from the few communal exercises we did attend that their discipline was strict. We were glad our superiors in our own order were a bit more lenient, and provided us a more cheerful atmosphere.

It was in our seminary days here that we were first exposed to a formal study of philosophy. We came to like it, because we felt it made us think and evaluate our attitudes.

Maybe we liked it because we had a great professor. Our philosophy teacher was Father Berkery, who was also our new superior. Father Berkery was a knowledgeable scholar and he was not afraid to expose us to other currents of thought. Father Berkery came to be the man who had the greatest influence on our lives, both in religious life and in our pursuit of the study and practice of folk music.

As our superior, Father Berkery was in complete charge of us. He taught philosophy at the college and at the same time directed our seminary. We admired him because he could laugh with us, tease us, and become involved in our lives, but he always retained his personal dignity and our respect. Like all great teachers, he was open to change and willing to learn from us, to understand us. He always made time for us, despite the press of his many duties. We marvelled at his wide range of experience. He had travelled extensively in Europe and he had published many articles on theology and philosophy.

Father Berkery believed with us that folk music could be a valid vehicle for religion and that through folk music, religion could find expression. Folk music, he told us, was the sum total of real experience, including religion, put to song. Father Berkery confirmed us in our belief that we had a valid concept of music as a medium for religion.

Father Berkery opened up for us a new and more intense understanding of religion. He helped us to become philosophers, as well as students of philosophy. His teachings were more than mere information about philosophy; rather they were living experiences in developing a philosophy. He helped us to understand and to feel the dignity of the human person. He helped us to know ourselves, to trust ourselves and our judgments. He gave us confidence in our viewpoints, because he respected what we said and thought. He made us constantly challenge and question, then to trust our direction. All these were new experiences to us, as they would be to all maturing young people.

Father Berkery made our work vital and attractive. He assumed that all his students were serious and capable, or else they should not be studying to be priests. And he believed a teacher should provide an atmosphere of creativity and responsibility.

Father Berkery was himself a real philosopher. He questioned *everything* but trusted *everyone* as a person. He questioned but he did not destroy. He consistently pointed up our responsibility to be creative and to summon up courage to take our direction from the deep resources within each of us, given by God.

He would not make philosophy a cushion for religion, for he believed religion should have the power to stand alone. And if a religion were unable to withstand the test of reason, then he rejected that religion as magic. His ideas and his approach were refreshing and stimulating. He instigated classroom discussions and he demanded that all of us take ourselves and each other quite seriously.

Father Berkery expected that we respond as mature men to his direction. He always demanded that we produce. He told us often that we had an obligation to rise from opportunity to achievement. He considered creativity almost an obligation of man. For him, life was a laboratory from which man must constantly learn, since nothing was really stable except our point of origin.

Through Father Berkery's guidance we saw religion as

life itself. He gave us deep insights into the Catholic Church and the human person. He encouraged us to take our music seriously. He drew us out, so that we might understand reasons for our belief that folk music could be a contemporary idiom to express genuine relationship with God.

Father Berkery greatly admired the late Pope John. The Pope's encyclical, *Pacem in terris*, was almost Father's rule book. Father Berkery succeeded in making Pope John's jovial and personal approach to God and life real for all of us.

Father Berkery showed us that a philosophical approach through inquiry was a valid path to creativity. He demonstrated how philosophy could deepen our own religious beliefs and at the same time make our religious message to others more sensitive and more contemporary.

Father Berkery helped us understand, through all we did, that we were brothers in Christ. We could sit down as one and share the beauty and the challenge of life. He showed us that our individuality was important and vital but at the same time he made us aware of our responsibility toward one another, and towards others. He made us sensitive to all people.

Christ was all important in Father Berkery's life and he wanted to be sure that we brought Christ into our own personal lives as fully as possible—in class, in music-sessions, in our everyday discusions.

In opening up the richness of our obligations to one another and to Christ, Father Berkery was not trying to make us deny our individuality as persons. Rather, he wanted us to see that the object of life is to live, enthusiastically, fairly, and completely.

"Responsibility," Father Berkery told us often, "is the important ingredient. Remember God and your commitment to mankind and responsibility falls into place. You'll find yourself able to respond, to give of yourself, to take defeat and success as they come along."

Because of our own self-disciplined work in our early music study while we were in the novitiate, we could easily accept the similar discipline of vigorous and exacting thinking demanded by Father Berkery. In fact, we really became quite impressed with ourselves; we considered ourselves quicker and more alert to philosophical problems. When we got into a discussion in or out of the classroom, we'd really consider it was our group teamed against the rest of the class. Others began to notice it. But Father Berkery was not a bit impressed.

At first, Father said nothing. But the next time we tried to steal the show he gave all of us a real run for our money. He didn't give us any chance to escape. He wanted to be sure we learned we were no different from others in the class; he wanted us to share the same advantages and the same handicaps. Father showed us we couldn't preach brotherhood and fairness if we ourselves were unwilling to practice these same virtues in our own lives. He made it clear to us that no one person or group could be outstanding unless he was willing to accept challenges and criticism.

From that moment on, we seemed to progress much more rapidly, probably, at least in part because our wings had been successfully clipped when our own sense of self-importance threatened to get in our way. Father Berkery always tried to temper our enthusiasm with realistic, penetrating insights.

We continued our studies, played our guitars, and delved deeply into our religious attitudes and experiences. We earnestly tried to separate emotional attachments from realistic understandings and insights. But we never had to be reminded that many others were making our success possible and that our lives themselves would need to be the real proving grounds.

During this period of our preparation, we also became volunteer orderlies at the county hospital. We learned to help people and we became sensitive to the suffering and pain of others. Although this kind of service meant we had to spend many late nights and early mornings there, we never regretted it.

Not too long after we started working at the hospital, Brother John O'Reilly, one of us, was the victim of a very serious accident. With the dedicated care of the hospital personnel (he suffered only a fractured clavicle) he was up and around before long.

Altogether, our half year in southern Missouri was a good one. We taught catechism to the grade-school children in Ste. Genevieve several times each week. This was quite a challenge for us, but one we gladly assumed. We ourselves were having difficulty accepting traditional explanations of our faith; now we were called on to make religion interesting and meaningful to a wide range of kids. Happily, we found our methods and explanations, as well as our folk singing, enthusiastically accepted.

We also entertained people in Ste. Genevieve County, and in the surrounding area. The people of Ste. Genevieve bought us a beautiful, new, bass fiddle to help out the sound of our folk music. Up to that time, we'd been using a battered reject.

We also made our first TV appearance around Thanksgiving time on a local variety show popular in the area. It was quite an experience and one that helped us project our musical message to a wider audience. Also, we were heard on local radio. In addition, we appeared before many parish groups, at local conventions, and even before several Protestant groups.

These many appearances gave us our first real taste of publicity. Because of changing ideas in the Church following Vatican II, people accepted us as part of that pattern of change. Many liked our material, and often publicity for our programs would appear in the local press. In general, critics were favorable.

Father Berkery was proud of us, as he was of all his seminarians. He wanted all of us to combine hard work, creativity, and responsibility with our music. "Without these," he would say, "you'll be either a failure, or at best, mediocre."

Father Berkery's influence on us became even more extensive as time went on. When he no longer had us as students, he continued to be the superior in charge of the seminary. He never ceased his direction and encouragement.

Four

After six months in southern Missouri, the whole seminary moved to the campus of St. Louis University, where we enrolled as regular college students in the spring term. We were impressed by the significance of this move. We would be one of the first seminaries in the country to study at a large metropolitan university.

But Father Berkery and other priests in our order realized some disadvantages. They knew that changes would need to be made in the kinds of control provided for us seminarians.

Of course, as students we could not know all that was involved in the move. But we were grateful that Father Berkery and others were willing to experiment, to help us make our experience at the University a rewarding one. We understood something of the problems faced in control and adapting to changing circumstances.

Our new home was a former hotel, then recently purchased and renovated by the Jesuits who leased different floors to various religious orders which were attending the University.

Quite a few graduate students also lived in the hotel. Our seminary was on the eighth floor. We heard many interesting stories about famous personalities who had once lived there. The glittering chandelier always looked lonesome hovering over the hundreds of seminarians who now swarmed through the halls.

Our move represented part of a change in seminary formation. It was a move toward giving future priests the experience of living in a bustling city. Seminarians would be offered rich opportunities for full development, intellectually and spiritually. St. Louis University ranks high among the nation's great centers of learning. Those who wanted to be priests in the order would most surely find their potential expanded. Isolation had been a weakness in previous seminary training. The seminarian was often shy and retiring, sometimes self-conscious, because his opportunities to mix with other groups had been limited. Living at St. Louis University gave us opportunities for expanded social association.

On campus, we were just another group of seminarians, out with our peers, jostling and hurrying each day with other religious groups, and with young secular men and women, many of whom were not even of our faith.

We were no longer required to wear black cassocks to class, although, of course, we had to dress neatly, and keep a fresh appearance. Living on the campus, we were living in a fish bowl. There were so many strangers moving about that we constantly had to look our best and do our best.

Getting adjusted to city life was difficult at first. After all, we had been living in the peace and quiet of the country where it was tranquil and restful. We had been the only ones in a large house. When tensions grew, it had been easy to snatch a few quiet moments on the large, surrounding grounds. Also, as in most small towns, none of us could go into town without some people calling out a cheery hello. Walking around a large city, we were just another part of the huge overflow.

Attending class at a big university was also different. Our daily attire was a Roman collar with black suits. We were easily identified as seminarians.

In class, we were expected to be prepared. We had to compete with our secular peers because now we no longer enjoyed the luxury of hiding behind our vocation or receiving special favors. We were forced to study, to meet the academic demands of the University. All this was helpful.

We did our best to enter wholeheartedly into the total life of the University. We realized we were a kind of pilot program and that other religious orders were watching, to decide whether to move to a campus, or to try still another kind of program. We felt it important to excel—and we did our best.

Many people think of a university as only classrooms or buildings with a campus and a library. We learned that a university is basically people, like a city itself. At St. Louis University we sought the best total education possible. For this reason we tried to involve ourselves in the whole life of the University, especially in extracurricular activities. We signed up for intra-mural sports, while at the same time we tried to make sure our grades did not suffer.

We also wanted to be sure we could give something to the University as well as take from it. We knew that good communication between seminarians and layman is vital.

We found we had free time on our hands, because we could arrange a schedule so that we only had to go to classes on Mondays, Wednesdays, and Fridays. The rest of the week was ours to use as we wanted. Also, our "seminary" in the hotel building was confining; we did not have the grounds we had previously, And the "hotel seminary" made no demands upon our time for housekeeping chores. While space and facilities were limited, curfew had been extended to at least eleven o'clock. All this meant that we had much free time.

Father Berkery knew we were young and active, and that we should not be so confined. At the daily Eucharist, Father Berkery hammered away at our serious obligation to offer mature response to our new responsibilities. He seldom refused us permission to go to a movie or for a drive. But he kept his message relentless and pointed: "Are you satisfied with what you do every day? Is this what you entered the seminary to do?" Two things helped us resolve the problem of free time: the inner-city, and self-awareness.

We had never been enrolled at a co-ed school before. Most of us entered the seminary when we were thirteen or fourteen. The seminary was a boarding school. We were allowed home for vacations during the summer and at Christmas. Seminarians did not date girls. It just wasn't done.

St. Louis University attracted its share of attractive young ladies. Could any of us *not* notice the girls, especially when we had seldom seen them at such close range before? Every time we turned around, it seemed we saw girls, girls, and more girls. In class, many sat next to us. We saw them on the streets, in the halls, on the stairs; and oh, what beautiful girls!

Father Berkery quipped: "They are here to stay; they're wholesome and they're human." He encouraged us to speak openly, and to express our feelings. "Don't ever be afraid to look at girls. If they're pretty, thank God for his genius. Don't ever close your eyes to God's handiwork."

We began to speak about sex quite frankly. We pulled few punches. We saw our vow of chastity as something positive, which did not restrict, but rather offered opportunity to mature.

"Love is not contrary to sex," Father Berkery said. Neither Christianity nor the priesthood are contrary to love. Celibacy is a private, personal choice. It must be freely made. But if you choose to forego personal sexual fulfillment, remember you do this in order to free yourself for more varied and deeper expressions of love. Your family, your interests, your service are broadened to include more persons. You do this through your personal sacrifice. Through your vow of celibacy you are able to reach out to a wider circle of people. You can help more people because you are not tied to only one. But celibacy is mature and the choice must be mature. This is why contact with the opposite sex is so important.

We realized that we would be playing with fire were any of us to date, and we would also risk the continuation of "our" experiment at the University. Father Provincial had openly stated that he would not hesitate to pull us out of the University and send us back to our former seminary if we abused the responsibility and trust given us. Some of us found difficulty in adjusting to a free and easy existence with co-eds, especially with free time on our hands. Were we serious about dedicating our lives to the service of humanity? If we were, we could not permit all our spare time to be filled frivolously.

In our community we set aside one day each month for meditation and reflection. This is called "retreat day." Its purpose was to refresh us spiritually. On retreat day, a visiting priest would deliver two or three long talks to the entire community.

One retreat Sunday, Father Berkery suggested we let the city be, in a sense, our "retreat master." He explained that any city street or area would tell us something, if we would only listen. "Go into the city," he said. "Find an area of real need. See if Christ is present there. And if he isn't, ask why not. Find out what you are prepared to do about it."

That particular Sunday was a cold day in early March. The air was biting, the sky was gray, and the wind churned around us. It was one of those days when one prefers to stay indoors and keep warm. Yet out into the cold we poured, making sure we first had a hearty breakfast. Father Berkery told us to come home around four o'clock, when we would all sit down and discuss our experiences.

We split up into small groups, converging on two main areas, a Negro ghetto and a white deprived area. We paired off, some going to each area.

What met our eyes that cold Sunday morning in March really shocked. We had all come from middle-class backgrounds; we had grown up expecting to be provided with a certain standard of housing and opportunity. Our general reaction was disbelief and dismay. The people we met were polite but distant. We admitted later that we all felt helpless in the face of the extreme poverty, suffering, and despair we witnessed first-hand that day.

We will never forget the poor, old lady, abandoned and sick, lying on a dirty cot in a freezing room, hungry and in pain, positive that no one even cared what happened to her. We can still see the crowded, one-room flats, the wood fires, the dirty, empty tables. We met lots of kids; *they* all ran to meet us. We saw dramatic possibilities to help, if only we could summon the courage to plunge in and try.

Wherever we went that day, we asked ourselves the same question: "Where is our Church?" We did see huge church buildings, once the pride and joy of a Catholic neighborhod, but now these were surrounded by broken-down buildings and overturned garbage cans. We wondered about ourselves, in our nice private, clean, carpeted rooms.

Christ was out there on those streets, all right. We saw him. But we saw a new picture of ourselves and none of us liked the picture.

We had taken a vow of poverty but we were not living it. What kind of witness to the poor or to the anxious were we? We worried about sex when real love was dying, when

one human being could ignore his brothers and wear a white-
wash for a collar.

We came home to the seminary that day changed men.
What we saw that day is burned in our memories. The day
was a most shocking experience. But we had to agree it was
the best and most realistic "retreat" we had ever made in our
lives. The images were hurting, hungry flesh; the "rhetoric,"
cold and calculating. We trembled as anger rolled through
our consciences.

Father Berkery had made his point. He had wanted us
to discipline ourselves, to move forward because of conviction, like responsible men. He asked us to rise to need
because we ourselves saw that need. And because he was
patient, because he had complete trust in us, he was able
to achieve his goals without compromising our dignity.

We went to bed that night chastened and challenged.
Father Berkery encouraged us to discuss our reactions to
our "retreat." Then he tied everything together. We who
were the folk singers, the message bearers, what were we
prepared to do now? We lay in bed, tossing and turning,
just thinking. If this Sunday were an awakening for us,
how many others who cannot walk through city ghettos
needed this also? Who would help these others discover their
brothers?

The next day Brother John spoke, and he spoke for all
of us. He asked us if we would seriously consider living and
working among the poor, taking our place where we be-
longed. "How can we," he asked, "sing about hunger and
cold, and men's hurt to each other unless we first experience
them? How can we be *real* folk singers otherwise?"

We still enjoyed watching the girls on campus, but we
were beginning to discover that our love and concern were
too much needed elsewhere to let them light on one person

alone. Time became a luxury, because so many other lives needed brightening and cheering, inspiration, and hope. Many of us soon took part-time jobs, running elevators late into the night, distributing phone books, acting as bartenders, and selling real estate. Others became cab drivers, messengers, or maintenance men.

We went down to the inner-city often. We did not live there full time yet, but at least we gave several hours of our surplus time each week. We were at last beginning seriously to become involved with the problems we had been singing about.

Five

Did we bring our guitars with us when we moved to St. Louis University from the old seminary? We sure did; we were eager to hit the concert trail! We placed great emphasis on the power of the concert stage because we felt we could reach many people and share our beliefs with them.

In the St. Louis area, people started to hear about us, and the demand for our music developed. We sought to make each concert different. We sang each song as if it were the first time we had ever done it. We really threw ourselves into our music so as to give the full meaning to the lyrics. Our songs were serious and at times heavy. So, in concert, we lightened our program with sing-alongs and light patter, parcelled into two forty-five minute periods with a fifteen-minute break. Someone once said that people love to sing when it's a song they can identify with or one they remember from a past period in their lives. So we always managed to slip a few of the old favorites into our repertoire and some fast-moving numbers that usually got people into the swing of things. After the performance, we went down to mix with the audience. We enjoyed these moments, using them to draw these people into serious conversation and comment; sometimes, we relaxed with our new friends.

Our audiences in general always seemed to enjoy our performances. When each show was finished, invariably some would come up to thank us and encourage us. Many said they never expected seminarians to be able to carry alone so long a program and still manage to get the audience to ask for more.

Our reputation grew and more and more requests for performances poured in. We sang before many kinds of groups, and usually were given a donation after a performance, but that part wasn't important to us. We sought an opportunity to get people to think and to care, and we were happy to tell them that we believed "sacred is the world." We frequently performed for hospital patients and for shut-ins.

We hoped, however, that somehow, someway, we would be able to reach a wider audience, and, perhaps, land a record contract with a major label. Realistically we realized that such a contract would be a path to greater influence, both in our Church and in society as a whole. We could demonstrate to the world that we had something to say, and that we could say it well.

One day a small article in the metropolitan paper caught our eye. There was to be a talent audition for a television show with the try-outs scheduled right on our campus. The article was passed to each of us. "Should we?" someone asked, with a smile. Finally we agreed: "Why not?"

We knew we might be criticized for auditioning. But if appearing on this television show would help us put our message before a wider audience, why not try it? Our singing was an important medium for us. Through it we felt we were able to communicate with the present-day world. Why should we hold back merely because some people might criticise?

The audition was an opportunity for a real break. It lighted up a path that we felt we inevitably had to follow. The program was designed specifically to showcase local campus talent, with one segment of the show being given to each of the colleges in the state.

The auditorium where the audition was to be held was jammed when we got there. Auditions had not yet started.

We filled out the necessary questionnaires. A man added our name to a list and gave us a time slot. "When you hear your name," he said, "move quickly, as we are running late." The atmosphere was impersonal and business-like.

Suddenly our name was called out. On the way up to the stage, we noticed that there were two other seminarian groups waiting to audition. One was a group of Jesuit singers. Our hearts dropped a bit when we saw them; we knew they were really good. The other group we didn't recognize. Anyway, we got on stage and sang one of our songs. A few seconds passed and we began to leave the stage, when a fellow in the aisles called out for us to do another number. Then we heard: "Okay, fellows, we'll be in touch with you."

We slipped off the stage as quietly as possible. In a few minutes, the Jesuit group came on; we stayed to watch and listen. But after *their* performance, we figured we'd better leave. We knew we couldn't win against that kind of competition. But at least, we had tried.

We went home and no one said much. Father Berkery asked how it went and we tried to explain. He wanted to cheer us up, but somehow it didn't work.

Two weeks later, John received a long white envelope from the company who had sponsored the audition. We had almost forgotten all about the thing.

Of course, none of us believed it. The letter had to be a mistake. But there was the row of neatly typed lines, accompanied by a check for one hundred fifty dollars! We had won after all! The taping of our segment was slated for that same week. The letter asked us to "try to be on time." Was there any doubt we would?

The taping went off smoothly and we were satisfied with the results. Photographers swarmed around the TV cameras and policemen kept the curious moving, for the taping was done out-doors, as still pictures were taken for the wire-services. Later that summer we watched the release of the show. It came over quite well and we were surprised and pleased. Independent stations around the nation picked up the tape and many of our friends in other cities watched the program. But the show did not specifically further our musical careers, although it gained us many new friends.

In and around the metropolitan area, we had adopted a habit of wearing a Roman collar. Usually seminarians are discouraged from doing so, for the collar is one of the outward signs of the ordained priests. Regulations at our university at that time required all seminarians to wear black suits, with either black shirt and Roman collar, or a white shirt with a black tie. We decided on the Roman collar because of practical considerations: in this way, one could easily and economically keep up a good appearance. Moreover, the collar was a tangible sign to the people in the inner-city with whom we worked.

One thing we found out by wearing "priest clothes" was that the knights of the road became our instant friends. Lots of them stay around the University, looking for a hand-out. They ask you for a quarter and promise you success in your exams and all kinds of prayers and good luck through all your life.

We obliged when we could, but since we often didn't have much money, at times we had to become hard-of-hearing. Especially was this true when there were three or more "knights" in a row. But usually we made a serious attempt to help, even if it meant giving up our lunch money, when things really looked bad. We tried to live what we believed —that all men are brothers.

One day, Jack was walking home when a tired, weary looking man put his hand on Jack's arm. Jack was startled; he stepped back quickly.

The man told a very sad story. We'll call him Peter James. He'd lost his baggage at the railroad station; he thought someone had stolen it. Could Jack possibly lend him enough money for a bus to Omaha? Over at College Church he had waited around to see a priest, he said. But the lady on duty downstairs chased him away. All he wanted was a few dollars and he would be sure to pay it back once he reached Nebraska.

Peter James was not an ordinary-looking man; he did not fit into the stereotype of a panhandler. He had deep-set eyes and looked very much a man who had just had a bit of bad luck. His clothes were clean, he spoke well with good vocabulary. He wasn't the smooth, smart, slick type. He seemed just a tired guy who had gotten a bad break. There was an air of credibility about him. Jack invited him to our seminary floor and the rest of us liked Peter right from the start.

Father Berkery put in a few phone calls to people Peter had suggested. He found out that Peter had been recently released from a rest home in New York, was fifty years old, and really had had more than his share of bad luck. He had been employed as a government missile inspector before he became seriously ill. But he had not really lost his luggage, he was just "on the road" trying to find someone who would give him a new start. His father lived in Maine and was unable to help him. His wife had divorced him. His daughter had just married and refused to allow him to come to the wedding.

Father Berkery agreed to allow Peter to stay with us a while. We got him a job running the elevator, then helped him find a small, furnished room nearby. We became fast friends. He had a charming way about him. Some of the stories he told were quite interesting.

Things seemed fine for a while. Peter had his job and

he seemed to be coming along. We had convinced him he ought to see a doctor and we were busy looking round for a better position for him. Peter made friends easily. He became a familiar sight around the halls of our hotel.

One night, as Peter was leaving to go home, a car turning the corner brushed lightly against him. Since Peter had a lame leg he lost his balance and fell to the pavement. He picked himself up without trouble, but he created quite a scene. Police rushed over; one of them hurried Peter to the hospital in a squad car. Peter made sure he got the driver's name and license and he also took down the policeman's badge and the number of the police report. He was taking no chances. The doctors at the hospital gave Peter a thorough examination and found only a slight bruise above his left eye. They sent him home, much to his dismay, making light of the whole affair.

Peter was determined to see "justice" done. He decided to sue the driver. He needed money, and besides, he had to justify in his own mind the gravity of the accident. He began a search for just the right attorney to represent him. He had lots of friends among the graduate students at the hotel, some of whom were enrolled at the University Law School. When he finished describing his accident, his injuries, and the doctors' sarcasm, the students sympathized with him instantly and one in particular promised to get him the services of the best lawyer in the city. Peter was happy.

A few days later, Peter came over to tell Jack he had at last got the name of a top-flight attorney and what was more, he had an appointment with him for the very next morning. He showed us the lawyer's card: James F. Gunn. "Did we know him?" Peter asked. No, we said, honestly. "Well that's strange," said Peter, "because his father is an important man in city politics."

Mr. Gunn and Peter met as planned the next morning.

After the meeting, Mr. Gunn talked to Father Berkery, since Peter had given him as a reference. He had already found out through quiet questioning something of Peter's background, but now he wanted to know what his connection was with our group. Together, Father and Mr. Gunn checked out the doctor's report. Gunn knew then he had no case.

Peter left us shortly after that. He finally did take a bus back to Omaha. We saw him in the area briefly a year later but he didn't stay around long. We had liked Peter, and tried our best to help him help himself, to restore a sense of dignity to his life. We were sorry to see him go.

The help that we initially gave Peter actually helped us, for it was Peter's attorney who adopted our singing group and managed it. Through his genius and insight, he guided us from a local group to one of the better-known folk groups in the nation. Without his expertise and know-how, we would never had dared to push on. Jim Gunn was the first layman to express a driving belief in us and our potential. He was the only one willing to invest time and money in us at the early stages of our development. Jim was a real friend right from the beginning.

Jim was a young and "up-and-coming" lawyer when we first met him. Well versed in the business of getting things done, he lost no time in putting some organization and direction into our group. Father Berkery visited him in his offices and explained what we were trying to do. They had immediate rapport; they spoke the same language and had similar measures of optimism and enthusiasm.

Jim promised to stop over at one of our concerts to see us in action. He came to hear us at an ecumenical "hymn-fest." Father Berkery was there, too, and the two men stayed after the show for a long and serious discussion of the group's future. Jim made up his mind that night that he would spare no effort to help us get moving; he became our first "manager."

He asked questions—loads of them. What efforts had we made to gain a national audience? How much money was needed to produce an album of original songs? How far was the group prepared to go? On and on went the searching questions, and we enjoyed every minute of it.

Jim is a no-nonsense man. When he sets his mind to do something, he gets it done—and done well. He had many contacts, and he knew how to put these to good use. He set up an audition for us with a man who had a daily radio show and we got a date to appear on it.

The program manager liked our sound. We had potential, he said. "But," he warned, "no one buys a pig in a poke. You must put out an album of original songs and the album must be done well, done professionally." He advised us to sink a lot of money into this attempt and promised us that it would pay off in increased opportunities. With a good album we would have something to put forward, something we could be proud of.

We were a bit disappointed, at first. After all, we already knew the bit about the album. We felt we were back where we started. We had expected to hear something different. He seemed to sense our frustration.

"Fellows," he said, "believe me. This is a rough business. Go to a first class studio, make the album at your leisure, but make it. If you do a good job, people will hear about you. This is the only way you'll reach people."

We left him and went home with Jim. We were more enthused now. A sense of urgency had gotten through to us. We saw that, really, our success was our own responsibility. We all headed toward Father Berkery's office, and sat down to begin another in a series of long discussions. We weighed the pros and cons of making an album. Were we ready? Did we have the right material? Who would help us? Could we obtain permission from our superiors in the order?

Finally Father Berkery spoke. He said that as far as the order was concerned, we could not count on any financial help. The community just did not have that kind of money to spare. But, he added, if the group raised the money itself, then the permission to make the album would be given. With that, we made our decision to go ahead on the album production. The die was cast. The month was June. The whole summer was ours; it lay wide open before us.

Within a week, Jim met with us again. "We're going to need at least a thousand dollars to get started," he said. "You'll have to get out and earn it yourselves. That means work and more work. Also, you'll need lots of practice. Studio time is expensive; you'll have to step up your practice sessions. Start getting the material ready, and fellows, you'll have to work like hell—excuse me, Father."

Jim was a hard taskmaster, but we were relieved to have someone like him managing us. He meant business. We set October as our target date for recording our album. In this way, we could take advantage of the Christmas audience.

We saw a lot of Jim from then on and became close friends with him and his family. He was not only our first manager, but he also became our attorney, looking after all the problems that lie in the way of any singing group with the hope of developing a national image.

Jim has become more or less one of our "family," and more like a brother to us than a business manager. We all fully appreciate how much he has given to our group and how much of our success is due to his initial encouragement and faith.

Six

Many people wonder why we sing, and why we have chosen to travel the Great White Way with our singing. We sing to tell the story of real people, real feelings—real despair, real hope, and real kindness. We sing to tell about life as millions live it—lest other millions forget.

Our Church, we feel, has often left thousands alone, for the most part seemingly forgotten. It has made it difficult for the poor and the disadvantaged to "identify" with it, because of its power and wealth. We sing to show that this is not really so.

John tells it this way:

If I were free to speak my mind, I'd tell a tale to all mankind of how I feel. The hurt I feel at the sight of a bleeding child. Compassion for the drunken mother who sits helplessly by. The void I feel for the father who never was. Disgust at the sight of broken wine bottles beneath a roach-ridden bed. The need I feel to think about it, pray about it, whisper about it, shout about it, and sing about it to anyone who could or should help me to help the helpless.

I feel like I'm watching a useless battle where friend turns upon friend, and the common flag is trampled under foot, because each refuses to see the need for the other. Where youth rebels against the spoon-fed values of the older generation, while the older generation itself is in doubt about the worth and value of its not too stable diet.

I see people who are afraid, scared to be themselves for fear of being hurt by others—who are more scared than they. Fear brings on confusion, mistrust, and stagnation. As I strain to understand it all, I can hear the suffering Christ calling out from this greatest agony, this most insidious evil, this darkness of fear.

I can hear him calling from the wayward delinquent who doubts if anyone cares whether he lives or dies. I can hear him calling in the drunken murmurs of the influential businessman who is trying to escape the shallowness of his mental bankruptcy.

But the fear cannot block out the good I can find in each of these individuals. This good is also the Christ calling to me, asking me to help make it grow. To call it what it is, so that this darkness and fear might be dispelled by the ever-present good Christ.

Here I am in 1969, studying to be Christ's minister, working even now to make him meaningful to people, working to make him real to people. I can't kid myself into thinking it is right for me to work with antiquated, obsolete tools, when everywhere around me, I can see a wealth of more useful instruments. I have to use tools that will do the job, that will bring Christ to the people and the world he made sacred with his blood. When I pick up a guitar, people sit down and listen. I have my chance to make my contribution to his cause. It works. So I'll continue writing songs and singing them.

I feel compelled to continue along this path, always remaining open to new and better ways of carrying out his mission. I've found my human vehicle in the group of which I am part, living and thinking, searching and singing, responding to one another's hopes and needs.

We will strengthen ourselves enough to stand for what we believe. To lead others who will look to us for guidance. To understand those who will look to us for compassion. We'll continue to grow, but in the ever-evolving, ever-progressing human, sacred world!

Jack puts it this way:

A few months ago, a thirteen year-old was sniffing glue. It wasn't the first time. It's really the only thing he has. Suddenly, he ran into my room, his small, frail body sweaty and seething. His mind was no longer in control as he darted around the room. I grabbed him and held him tight. I can still remember seeing him, as he tried to wrench himself from my terrified grasp. He swung towards the wall and began pounding and swinging madly. He was muttering something about killing Steve. I know Steve, too. He had gotten our thirteen-year-old's mom pregnant. Let's call the young lad, Fred.

Fred is one of five children, four of whom sleep in a single room. The house needs someone to keep it clean and cozy. Fred knows the family has little money but he can't stomach his home turning into an open house for strange men. I never really knew before that a thirteen-year-old could resent this. The glue brought out his feelings to me.

It was during that nightmare, as I wrestled with that writhing, tortured young life, that my own life became more meaningful. Fred wanted to take a life. Instead, he helped me to a deeper life, if only because I was forced to care.

Previously, I often wondered what life was all about. Why was I alive? Why did I come to the seminary? I searched, and everything seemed general and abstract, so distant. Nothing seemed real. But when I held Fred, I was hit by real need. Perhaps before I had never reached out to need. This time, need, dreadful need lashed itself around my very person. I had to respond. Before, I was always so busy, wrapped up in myself, distracting myself in a search for answers. I couldn't see the beauty of a real, human person who could lift himself up if only I would help.

I have come now to a much deeper understanding and appreciation of other persons, through my work in the inner-city and especially with my religious community, The Contemporary Mission. Now I know that today's seminarian must be concerned. He must be able to not simply look, but also to see. He cannot just hear, but he must listen. He must not just say, but also do. This is why I have dedicated my life to opportunity, risk, and achievement.

What do I want now out of life? I want other people to listen. God has blessed me with so many opportunities to help my fellow man. Now I want to share those opportunities. Helping others is really helping yourself to a richer life.

I know that in the past I haven't always responded to the challenge of achievement. Sometimes I have failed; at times, I have failed miserably. But kids like Fred can't take any more failures.

This is why I want to sing. I want to share what I have learned. I want to tell the world that "There'll Come a Day" when four children won't have to sleep in a filthy bed, when nine and thirteen-year-olds won't have to blot out their lives in a lethal mist of glue.

I want to tell the world of my experiences with the poor, the lonely, the suffering, the forgotten, the unknown.

Joe says:

Once I wrote a letter to our University paper, criticising a protest vigil that had been held on campus. Several months later, a priest who had read the letter came up to me and said, "Joe, ever since I've read that letter, I've been looking for you." I almost felt like answering back, "I've been looking for myself a heck of a lot longer than that!"

It's true. I've spent a great part of my life waiting for the real Joe to please stand up. If I'd kept on waiting, I might still be watching the world pass by, for I expected to find myself as a person apart, a person singularly blessed, who would somehow find a way to help fallen mankind. I must admit, it would have been a hard search.

As time went on I began to realize that the young men with whom I'd been living for several years were making their own same search. At the time, I didn't fully appreciate what I was doing, but I joined with them. I made my first new friends, and we continued our search together.

That was only a few years ago, but since then I've gone a long way toward knowing myself, but I've also been given the chance to show others "the way."

This is what my singing means to me. I've always made my own contributions to the work of the group and to the albums we've recorded, but the scales show I've received more than I've given, and I've learned more than I've taught.

I've received confidence in myself; that tells me I *can* contribute to the world I live in. It has taught me, also, that I have a responsibility to make these contributions.

All the talk in the world won't make me or my neighbor a better person. Actions speak louder . . .

I've also received the chance to develop my own ability to create. Every person has some originality. Mine is imagination. But I've learned to be unafraid of mistakes. Mistakes are the way by which we learn and grow.

Most important of all, my singing has helped me develop real concern for others. This is why I continue with The Mission, for through song I can, with my friends, communicate this concern to those who want their interest to grow. I've seen what Christian concern has done for me in my life. I see this concern expressed in our singing. I want to see this concern in the lives of those whom I meet.

Don explains:

Understanding another man's point of view, respecting that man for what he is as you would want him to respect you, this is for me the essence of living. Sparked by Christian commitment, it is a life which cannot be lived on the surface only. Its foundations must run deep but never silent.

We of The Mission really believe in one another. We base our friendships on complete honesty with, and open trust in, one another. Because of this we can share ideas and experiences; we enjoy a unity of ideas and ideals. Unity, not unanimity, is what aids us in the performance of work to fulfill our apostolate.

What has all this to do with our life in the inner-city? It's really the shared experience, the atmosphere of trust within, that forms the nucleus from which our work grows and matures. We try to live our ideals on our home ground, to communicate them more effectively in our music.

I spent several years in the military service, so I guess you could say I've "been around." I've seen life in some of its more raw aspects. I hardly consider myself really an idealist. But in the service, I learned to survive with my ideals pretty well intact and did my best when called upon, but I wasn't always too eager to heed any call, except mess and duty.

I've changed since those days. Since I joined The Mission, I've begun to see my Christian faith as a challenge, because I've been placed right in the center of real suffering and deprivation. I can't pass the buck anymore. My hands and even my total person I consider the really last resort these people have. If I—and others like me—turn away, what happens? When I entered the seminary, I chose to become a promise of better things for all my brothers. I must respond now. And it's a funny thing; I not only really don't mind it at all, it's my whole life.

Perhaps the actual experience of living with being buried in the realities of deeply agonizing human problems forces us to cry out for help. What we see is not fair. This cannot be the triumph of technology, science, medicine, of the total of civilization. Christianity *cannot* turn away and pretend everything's just fine.

That's why we sing. We want everybody to know about the thirteen-year-old boy who attempts to escape the horrible reality of his own existence by sniffing glue fumes. We want everybody to know about the young mother attempting to hold together a family which has not known a father. We are not the apostles of the bleak and the black, only. We are not *blaming* anybody. We just know that lots of people need help. This is why we sing. We hope that those who *can* love *will* hear, and come forward.

What does the future hold? What tomorrow brings depends much upon today. We all need to become concerned and sensitive. The message of our lives and of our singing needs a response. The response must come from all who desire to make a better world.

Rats, disease, chains, tenements, loneliness, drunks—who can live with these every day? Who wants to even talk about it? Poverty hurts. It shrivels. Most people like to forget it.

But someone has to remember. It's not right: all those kids, all those people—and no escape routes. Will a day ever come?

Hope swirls out through lonely chimneys. Who cares? Outside the poverty pockets, people seem to say, "That's too bad, there's nothing we can do."

We sing because we don't want to forget, and because we don't want others to forget there *is* something that can be done. We sing so that the other people will hear about the great need and the burning opportunities to do something about that need.

Seven

"Where can we get a record of yours?" "Don't tell me you don't have an album out?" There were constant questions at our concert appearances. At that time, we had no record contract. We certainly had no album.

People who had helped us in our music career continued to urge us to record ten or twelve of our songs, and let that be our platform. They urged us to think of an album. Father Berkery didn't push us—but he didn't stop nudging us, either.

In late August we moved again, this time to a complex of ramshackle tenements. People were still living in some of these apartments but once they were all moved we were going to use them as a new seminary.

We left our quarters in the hotel building mainly because the rent there was just too high for our small order. But the seminary enrollment was now past thirty, and rather than pay money into rent for this size group, Father Berkery decided to put us in a more realistic kind of seminary building. At the same time, he would be saving money for the order.

Our new home was very close to the University campus, and near one of the most beautiful and graceful streets in the city. It is close also, to the site of the new St. Louis Cathedral and the beautiful Chancery building.

Our move didn't cost the order much, for the buildings were in pretty poor condition. But all thirty of us painted, scrubbed walls, panelled, and moved donated furniture inside. When we first moved in, rats, roaches, and floor rot lived side by side with us. But eventually, all of us overcame our initial reluctance. We found out what a difference can be made with hard cleaning and lots of elbow grease.

Our new home put us within a five-minute walk of the University. It also put us right into an area of genuine need. The people around us had very little of anything. Most of the people around us were poor but they were at least employed somewhere. Few seemed to be actually as deprived as had some of the people whom we had worked with in the hard-core poverty areas. The neighborhood was a blighted area but it seemed much better than some in the city.

One night a man who ran a music studio a few blocks away dropped over to meet us. Father Berkery had invited him to dinner. We were all glad of the chance to have someone like Oren Brown review our songs and, maybe give us some coaching, especially since we were scheduled to record in Chicago in only two months.

Oren was a quiet type of person. He spoke deeply, slowly, precisely. He listened intently to our plans. Then he asked us to go through a few numbers for him. He sat quietly. It was difficult to sense his reactions. Finally, looking over his joined hands, as though hoping his words wouldn't hurt us, he spoke.

"Fellows," he said, "I charge a lot, but I'm good. So you can be sure you're getting the best." He continued: "I like your voices but I must tell you quite frankly that you need a lot of training, especially in fundamental principles, such as breathing, pausing, spacing, phrasing. I like your sound and your songs. I believe you have something. These deserve good coaching. I feel sure I can give you the best training available." We didn't have much money; that was always our problem. But he agreed to take us as a group, at a reduced rate.

The next day our first professional coaching experience was under way. We practiced at his studio several hours each week. Then with Jim Gunn as an audience we would continue practicing far into the night. With each day, pressures developed and tensions grew. Reality was hitting home. These songs we now merely practiced would soon be locked within the grooves of a recording—our first album—and we just had to give our best.

We put in lots of time in rehearsals. But we also had other commitments. The new seminary building required constantly more and more attention. Also, classes at the University would start again, shortly. All of us had become involved with people in the inner-city during the past summer and we could not let these friendships die with the fall—even with our first album just ahead.

We spent a lot of time in Father Berkery's apartment, since he had the only large room in the seminary where all of us could fit. We tried to do our part to plan and furnish the rooms in the seminary. One of us designed the community chapel. Others got themselves involved with paint and clean-up jobs.

Father Berkery helped us with our songs, and guided us in the thinking and planning of our promotional literature. He listened to our experiences in the slum areas. He allowed us responsible freedom, and we were never at a loss for ways to put this freedom to use. Father desperately wanted us, as he wanted all his seminarians, to succeed; he realized how much our ideals meant.

Most of the seminarians liked the openness of the new training system. They liked being permitted to come and go freely. But Father Berkery was not completely permissive. He demanded that all of us produce, that we give of ourselves. He required that we respond in a sensitive way to the needs surrounding us.

Most people accepted our work. But many priests and even some seminarians didn't consider it as proper. But Father Berkery approved. "Fellows," he would say, "your worth to the Church and to your community is in direct proportion to your contribution in production. You must make responsible use of your freedom; you have received a blank check from me. The rest is up to you. How can I help you further? Tell me, convince me, and I'll help. But if you're here for a free ride, get off now."

Many in the seminary resented us. But those who were honest, who were themselves involved in an apostolate, who knew how to grow with the new framework of freedom, trust and responsibility, these men were our good friends.

Jim Gunn was a frequent visitor these days. He had just returned from Chicago where he had mapped out a strategy for us. One night he called us to come to his home for a special briefing session. He asked us to do for him the twelve songs we had finally chosen for our first LP. Then he broke the news.

Six hours of studio time at a prime Chicago location had been reserved. Jim went over basic costs involved in this recording project. Printers had been contacted to make up the album cover in black and white—color was out of our price range. Pressing and packaging would be done by RCA. Our timetable called for the Christmas market.

We were greatly pleased. But the reality of it all made us tense. Jim said we needed more practice sessions, so we were working at it into early morning hours. Also, we had to come up with a title and design the jacket. Father Berkery agreed to write up the notes for the back of the record sleeve. John came up with a good idea for the front cover design, so he was given the green light on that part of the job.

We all realized the importance of this first album. Here

was the best vehicle we had ever had for putting our message across to a wider audience than we would have dreamed possible. The album cover just had to be right. We wanted it to symbolize in a graphic and exciting way our message and our goals.

Most of the songs for the album had been written by either John or Joe. One song was entitled, "There'll Come a Day." It has a catchy melody; the lyrics ask questions, burning questions about the bomb, people, and suffering, and through it all ran a vein of hope. John suggested this be the title of our new album: *There'll Come a Day.*

To gather necessary illustrative material for the cover, John asked a crack photographer from the diocesan paper to spend a day with him in the slums. There they captured real moments in a present-day ghetto, made poignant by kids, with seminarians, flickering neon lights, and snatches of darkness. From these photos, John created a montage, and across the suffering faces of trapped humanity, we scattered the letters of our title: *There'll Come a Day.* Our first album cover was off the drawing table. It was not a professional job but it told a true story, wildly and with a roar.

On the last of October, we left for Chicago. The St. Louis superior of the Servite priests, who was a close friend of ours, arranged with his order's motherhouse in Chicago to reserve rooms for us at the Servite monastery near the Loop. Jim Gunn was with us and also Oren Brown, our vocal coach. They wanted to be sure that our singing was at its best.

When we look back over our first recording, we're amazed at our brashness and naiveté. But our lack of professionalism worked in our favor. We arrived at the studio with not the slightest knowledge of the mechanics involved in making a recording. We were not at all prepared for the maze of microphones, the many technicians and the problems of multiple retakes. We were our own instrumentalists and our own vocalists. The engineers were patient; they had recorded folk singers before, so they were not too dismayed by our constant tuning of guitars. Nor did they become upset at the "cuts" shouted out in the middle of almost every song. They just smiled and we started all over again. But, with bleary eyes, we watched the relentless clock, knowing that each take cut deeply into our limited funds. We had just six hours and we just about made it. As we look back upon it, it seems pretty close timing, to record twelve songs.

We had recorded on four tracks, so, next, the engineers had to produce one master tape from all four. This technique, called mixing, was something we knew nothing about, then. So when the engineer offered to let us help him with it, we passed up the opportunity. Since then, we've found out that mixing is one of the most important steps in the making of a recording. If it is not done well, an album will be ruined.

Two weeks after the recording sessions, the acetates, which are a kind of proof-copy of the album, arrived. Jim set up his portable stereo and folks we had invited in listened. The guitars and our voices came over crystal clear; this was the sound of The Mission.

As each song came through, we began to feel better and better. We found our first LP album quite satisfying, so much so that we spent that night and the early morning listening and relistening to each sound. We knew we had a long, hard road before us. But the worst seemed over. Jim and Oren were not professionals, but through their dedicated work, support, and encouragement, they had managed to make it possible for us to come through with a product that would effectively project our philosophy and our beliefs.

It was three weeks before Christmas. The completed albums had not yet arrived. Phone call check-ups gave the

earliest release date, now, as the coming February. There
was a backlog of over six million albums, we were told. By
this new release date we could surely never make any
Christmas mailings; we would be fortunate to make Easter!

Father Berkery called the floor director of the press
plant. He told him how much this album meant to us, and
how important it was to receive at least a part of our order.
Could we get five hundred or a thousand, Father asked?

The floor director promised to see what could be done.
He called the next day to tell us we could get five hundred
stereo and monaural albums, if someone could go over to
pick them up.

John and two others were practically on their way before he hung up and they returned the next day with our
prize. We thought the finished album was excellent. We
were more than happy. One song seemed to be a favorite
of radio stations. We seemed to hear it everywhere:

How many years, Lord, how many days
Can the world go on this way?
How many battles, how many wars
Can bring that peace we're lookin' for?
Oh, there'll come a day, when hatred will cease
And all the world will have peace, oh Lord,
*And all the world will have peace.**

**Copyright, Archway Music Co., New York. All rights re-
served.*

Eight

All through college we took our studies very seriously and achieved good grades. We were often asked how we found time to keep up our class work and our music, as well as working with the disadvantaged.

Perhaps part of the answer is that we always kept ourselves aware of our goals. We wanted to be priests as well as informed individuals. That meant we had to budget our time carefully.

We planned open-end discussions during our study periods where we could talk over and exchange ideas about particular assignments. Our evenings were filled visiting poor families, working with kids, or rehearsing our music. In the winter, we often found time for indoor sports.

The only unscheduled time we allowed ourselves was our individual study hours, although sometimes we had a free weekend. These times we usually used to catch up on some library assignment, or to complete other obligations of our University classes. We loved to keep busy and active. Even when we reached Divinity School, which as a graduate school has fewer required classes or lectures, we followed much the same schedule.

We like to read, and therefore, library assignments hold no terrors for us. Like most young people, we like to be out on the sports field, but we also enjoy the time we spend on our studies because we know how necessary these will be to our priesthood.

Our social life at college was not overlooked. We knew

that a man studying for the priesthood, like everyone else, needed time to relax. Although, or perhaps because, God is and will always be part of his life, the seminarian should not abstain from ordinary, healthy fun. We know that to be Christian means also to be fully human.

Of course, having freely chosen celibacy, we didn't date. We did not join in any activities which would be contrary to the behavior of a future priest. We tried to choose carefully the occasions to which we lent our music. Once we were asked to sing at a draftcard burning ceremony, and we turned it down, because we felt that when one dissents it should be done positively.

God has been very good to us and life is very real to us. We would never knowingly go against his will in any way. We may make our share of mistakes, but we always make every effort to live by the rules and principles we feel to be correct. We know that the popularity and acceptance of any seminarian groups stem as much from their devotion to their basic philosophy of life and to their convictions. In our case, only in a secondary way did it stem from our music.

The need to dedicate oneself to an idea is very important. To achieve one's goal, he must concentrate all his actions toward that goal. Sometimes, he must forego some things, to conserve his time so that he can achieve what he wants. Sometimes, some tasks may seem useless or trivial, but if they contribute to his progress toward the goal, they become worthwhile.

So, the real answer to our ability to combine academic work with helping the disadvantaged is found in one word: dedication. No amount of mental ability or musical talent would by itself help us without dedication.

Some people find their inspiration in quiet places, with tall Gothic spires. We drink up inspiration and energy from God's poor—the lonely, the rejected, the disadvantaged.

These represent God for us. We carry this awareness of God with us whether on the concert stage or in the classroom. This awareness of the need of others for us gives us confidence. We know many people depend on us, and how important our total success is to them. This spirit of dedication and awareness helps us overcome many obstacles. Without it, our devotion to study and to music would become worthless.

Nine

Record contracts are not handed out on the basis of one's own evaluation of his performance. We always thought our singing was pretty good and that we had something different to offer, musically. But convincing a major record company to take a chance on us was more difficult than we had thought.

We made the rounds of several record companies in New York; in fact, we went back to them again and again. The days were filled with phone calls, letters, auditions, plane flights—exciting, powerful stuff for us. But most of the companies hesitated to make any commitment to us. A half year after our first album was released—June—we had managed to convince two national companies that we had something positive to offer them. But we were later to regret our final choice.

One was a company which had given us the nod when most people wanted none of us. The other was a large company with name recordings to its credit. But it was one of those who could never find anyone to listen to us, earlier. The first company had a reputation as a "blues outfit," with mostly Negro and "soul artists." Since then, however, this company has skyrocketed to become one of the hottest labels in the industry. Unfortunately, *that's* the one we turned down and we took the big-name. It proved too big and too "posh" for us to refuse.

After driving through the snail pace of busy New York traffic on a hot summer afternoon, we found the air-conditioned office of the company to be a pleasant change. Also, we were in good spirits; we were about to sign an exclusive contract with a large New York booking agency. We hoped in this way to broaden our potential by breaking into the college concert circuit.

Many had told us that our concerts were a natural for college audiences. In fact, in the Midwest area this had seemed to us to be true. College kids seemed to like our lyrics. This booking agency specialized in college concerts, and also signed artists for television shows and other types of public appearances.

Our contact at the booking agency was a one-time musician himself. We felt surely he must have ulcers because he was always on the phone arguing with a client or trying to work a better "deal." His constant companions seemed to be cigarettes and coffee, with a dash of chicken soup thrown in for variety.

When we first met him, he was in conference with another singing group made up of young fellows around our age. He set up an audition, then stated he felt he could easily place us, and signed us. He told us about the many places he could book us, like the Forest Hills Festival, the Rheingold Festival in Central Park, Carnegie Hall, and on and on. But we soon found that he promised more than he could deliver. He was a nice guy but he had a terrible memory. He promised the world to everyone but forgot which part he promised to whom. In the beginning, however, it was great to hear about all the possibilities that did exist.

An agent receives a 10 percent fee. When the agent heard we had obtained a record contract by ourselves, he was amazed. But he thought, however, it would be more to our advantage to sign with a "prestige label," as he phrased it. His arguments made sense, but we didn't see how we could get still another company interested in us when we had a contract with one. He promised to set up another audition, that very afternoon and bring the vice-president of Warner Brothers to hear us.

We did our new song, "Yesterday's Gone" and a few others. The VP listened, then said, "I like it. You have a great sound. But I'll have to check with the coast. I'll let you know."

We were not about to wait for another two weeks. We felt we could afford to turn him down; the contract from the other company was in our pockets. We said rather than wait, we'd sign with the other company the next day. The VP saw we meant what we said. He made a quick call to the coast and got the authorization he needed to sign us immediately to an exclusive contract with his company. We finally decided to sign with Warner's.

Agents are very necessary, but an agent is not a personal manager. We had earlier considered whether it might be wise to have a personal manager. Both men—the agent and the VP—discouraged the idea. Later, we found out why. A personal manager becomes the direct representative of the performer. He merchandises the act; he "sells" it to people who count. A good manager works miracles. He taps every possible resource for the performer. The main avenues of every artist are the record company he is signed with and the agent who books him. So it was understandable that both the record company and the agency would discourage us from engaging a personal manager.

An agent works somewhat like a storekeeper. When a TV studio, or a producer, needs an act, he calls the big agencies and they try to find what is needed.

Personal managers are architects. They are creative, while agents select and make appropriate services from among many. Our booking agency is a huge organization. It had thousands of performers among its subscribers. It cannot serve only one person or one group to the detriment of others. An agency must be organized for profit, as is all business. We were fortunate to find an agent who was unusually generous and kind. We knew we were lucky.

Our new company didn't believe in wasting time. We'd have to get out a new album that summer, the VP told us, for definite release in the fall. We were weary after our numerous visits, trying to land a contract. We felt we needed a few days to rest up before recording sessions. Warner Brothers agreed, but told us we'd really have to push; there was a lot to be done, with rehearsals still to be scheduled and held. Then the VP told us he had obtained for us the perfect musical director.

Milt Okun was tall and quiet, very much at home with sheet music before his eyes and sounds in his ears. We had known his musical arrangements when we first started singing together and we were his ardent fans. He had always enjoyed folk music and he had arranged for many of the prominent performers. When our new company suggested Milt, we knew we wanted him.

He gave us an appointment the next day. He asked for a copy of our first album and listened right there to one cut. Then he asked some of us to sing for him, just so he could get the feel of our group.

Milt worked with us day and night in the following weeks. He was not at all difficult to work with, although he was quite firm. He seldom lost his temper and our practice sessions under his direction were always interesting and productive. He was "just the man for people who love to live their work."

Now that we had signed with a large record company, we had a professional company with massive promotional resources to push our recordings. This sounds great on paper, but in reality, we weren't satisfied. We felt our music could have been promoted more widely than it was. We were inclined to agree with one of the secretaries who believed that her company "appeared all thumbs" as far as giving us real promotion.

The hard truth was that the VP who had signed us did not have much authority. The "men on the coast" were the top brass, and they did not really know us, nor did they understand too well what we were trying to do.

Despite what seemed to us poor promotion, our first album with this company, *Yesterday's Gone*, sold quite well. One of the coast executives told us they were very pleased, and looked forward to a profitable relationship with us. Really, the album did well because we promoted it ourselves. We felt it carried our message, and we wanted that message projected well and effectively.

Many people helped us promote the album. One to whom we owe a lot managed an outdoor advertising company, which donated fifty large-sized billboards to us and we used them to advertise our album. Other companies across the country donated additional outdoor ad space. Altogether, we had over 500 large billboards spotted across the country.

In addition to the donated advertising, we went on a small promotional tour, at our own expense, to several cities in the Midwest, and to New York. At each we asked top radio stations to play one of our singles, *Yesterday's Gone*. Many went all out for us, so much so that in one month's time *Yesterday's Gone* was played on the air over five thousand times.

Thinking back, we consider that Warner Brothers was good for us. The company gave us a break, and for that we are grateful; but the agency, despite its good will and interest, never really panned out for us. Maybe we expected too much.

Ten

The successes we had earlier meant little now that we were signed to a major national recording company. Now, instead of being at the top of the local ladder, we were starting over again nationally. We promised ourselves to follow the same route as we had in the past. We would continue hard work and practice, we would continue to dedicate ourselves to our goals and above all, we would never neglect our first obligation to training for the priesthood.

We knew that the demands upon our musical training necessary to fulfill our contract commitment would make it more difficult to discipline ourselves scholastically. But we had sought a contract with a major recording company to further our professional music careers. So we set out to reach the goals this contract offered us: a chance in the professional world of music, and improved training that would better equip us for professional performances.

We felt we had done a good job as amateurs but we did not know how well we'd do in the big time. Our musical director knew that many new groups felt this way, so he set about to restore our self-confidence.

He meant a great deal to us and we respected and admired him. His encouragement was just what we needed and it wasn't too long before he shaped us into a good performing group.

We walked into the recording studio on a warm day in August and were happy to see so many of our friends there to encourage us. This session was but the first of more than six. Each day we were boxed up in the glass booths of the studio, singing, playing, repeating, sweating. Photographers came and went, followed by newspaper reporters, all interviewing us, while all the time we worked madly to get the right sound on tape.

Our album of eleven songs was completed in about three weeks, climaxing a grueling period of work, but which left us a treasury of experiences. To celebrate the completion of the album, the company took us out to a wonderful dinner at a little Italian restaurant.

The next day we needed to be up before dawn to pose for pictures for the album cover. Just to be sure we were on time, we arrived early and had to wait almost an hour for the photographer. The finished product can now be seen on the cover of *Yesterday's Gone.* Somehow, it makes all the early rising and hard work that went into it well worthwhile.

With the recording sessions completed, we headed home for a round of local TV appearances and more concerts. We were completely tired out but we felt a real sense of accomplishment.

With the new term, we enrolled in the newly founded Divinity School of St. Louis University. We were beginning the final phase of our preparation for the priesthood. But we were still four years from our goal. The Divinity School offered high hopes but we found that most of the courses were much the same abstract theory we had known previously. Still, all of us enrolled there, Jesuits and other orders hoped the new Divinity School would provide new, creative programs of priestly formation. The original plans for the School included links with Protestant and Jewish seminaries in the area, and this we looked forward to.

It was difficult to keep our minds on classes now. Our experience in New York had left its mark. But we had little choice other than to settle down, for the seminary training was our primary obligation and everything hinged on our being successful in it.

We were now living full-time in a white poverty pocket of the city. We wanted it this way, so that our recording successes would not divorce us from the crying realities that gave substance to our songs. We continued to work with the young people in our area and often we spent much of our time talking with the older folk; somehow everything fell back into place; we were home again and we were content.

Just about that time a young producer for CBS came out to film our work and concerts and to interview us. He was a very sincere person and we enjoyed working with him. He seemed to really capture the spirit of our work. Through filming that session we found out filming a television show requires countless hours of work as well as great skill and precision. But when we finally saw the finished program we were astonished at the art the producer and director had employed. No one would ever suspect the tremendous efforts by all of us that went into the making of "Sacred is the World."

We had previously been guests on local TV shows but now such opportunities were even greater. Through these appearances we made new friends, all of whom helped us with our musical careers. People took our work more seriously now.

Our new album, *Yesterday's Gone*, finally arrived. Again, people crowded into Father Berkery's office to hear it. As we listened to it, we knew our musical director had done a great job. The songs really sounded professional. The album was a good showcase of our work.

Reactions poured in from everywhere. Our single,

"Yesterday's Gone," was picked as an instant hit. Our album was cited "must play." The trade magazines spoke of a "new folk-rock style." They were enthused.

Our director, Milt Okun, long-distanced that now we had to hit the concert trail. This was the price one paid for a booming album but, then, this was also what we were looking for when we sought to make the recording. He arranged several appearances.

One of them was in Chicago on a lonely Thanksgiving Day. We were first on the program. We appeared before an audience of more than eight thousand people and to say the least, we were scared. We performed in our Roman collars and black short-sleeved shirts. The audience seemed pleasantly surprised and we appreciated their bursts of applause, responding with two encores.

Our Chicago concert was very important to us. We knew we were being watched, for style, projection, and audience reaction. We had chosen to compete on a truly professional level, and if we went over well, we would have more such opportunities. We made it; certainly, this appearance was one of the most important and rewarding of our lives.

Earlier, when we had returned from New York, we were knee-deep in music, and singing had become the center of our lives. There was absolutely no doubt in our minds that the talents God had given us must be used to help underprivileged and abandoned peoples. We were not certain where God would lead us in the future; we expected it would be ever more challenging. We felt we were called on to explore new dimensions. If publicity and fame came, these would have to be used for the good of mankind. God wanted us to witness for him. He was opening up for us a career that would help us win the respect of thousands and in this way we would be able to share our message with them. We believed this honestly and completely. With the increase in our national acceptance as a musical group, our sensitivity to the demands of our vocation to the priesthood heightened.

During the following weeks we sang for many groups and our message was always the same: no man is an island; we need one another; we are all brothers; with a proper knowledge of Christ, you can have a fuller, more intense, more meaningful life, whatever your chosen work may be.

Our work with young people brought us fulfillment and, from them, enthusiastic response. At any local high school concert, we were usually asked for repeated encores. The teachers found our approach interesting, and many asked if we had any written materials available that they could use in the classroom. They urged us to write such materials, because they saw we caught the interest of young people, that we could get them thinking about serious issues, such as poverty, civil rights, war and peace. If we could find some way to a more permanent and broader influence in the classroom, they could see more advantages. Such demands as these became more urgent and more frequent as time went on, so one day we began to brainstorm.

Father Berkery came up with the idea. He suggested we write a discussion booklet, using our songs as a base around which to initiate dialogue. This proved to be a natural, since we had written our own songs. We were looking for something easy to put to use in the high school classroom yet interesting enough for adult groups as well. We decided to link up our songs with current happenings, and select headlines from local newspapers to stimulate discussion. And so we launched our writing careers, as usual under the careful eye of Father Berkery, himself the author of a book called *Restructuring Religious Life*, published by Alba House. His book sold over eight thousand copies in less than one month. This is quite a feat considering that Catholic publishing houses count a three thousand sale as a best seller.

We started to work on our new project with our first album. First we put out a folio, with words and music, and with a series of interesting photos that seemed to best catch the theme of the songs. This we had printed ourselves. Then we started on the discussion booklet. We tried to press into it all the meaning from the lyrics and to dress up the package attractively.

When we thought we had something good, Father Berkery and John took our materials to a publisher. Father explained the project to the editorial director who liked the idea. Discussion groups on current problems were mushrooming throughout the nation and there was a great need for teaching materials. The publisher finally accepted our materials, entitling them *Dialogues in Self-Fulfillment*.

The editor's decision proved sound, judging from the enthusiastic reception given both the album and the discussion booklet by the country. Here again, we were broadening our influence and in this way moving closer toward the achievement of our goal: helping religion and music work hand in hand for the dignity of man.

Our discussion booklet was a first stepping-stone for us in the literary field. Also it opened the door of many classrooms and homes to us. Through the booklet we were brought to the attention of the Center for Media Development, a creative, literary organization. One of the two men who managed the organization explained what they had in mind for us. Their company had just signed a contract with several recording companies to develop an audio-visual program for schools using the music of a well-known Negro singing group. Through the appeal of this group, who were idolized by the teen-agers, an attractive educational and health program was being produced. The company wanted to make use of the broad appeal of our group in a similar venture. The program would be planned for us in guidance and in social study groupings. The company wanted to make use of our music and of our actual experience in working with the disadvantaged, to stimulate a social conscience in young people, in both public and parochial schools. The Center planned to develop and produce an entire audio-visual program in this way. The name of the program was to be *Insights.* We were delighted with this new opportunity to expand our influence by contributing effectively to changing educational needs.

More than anything else, we wanted to serve man, to share our faith in human dignity and to witness the real Christ of the Gospels, wherever and whenever we could. This desire was immeasurably stronger than even our desire to sing or write, although we recognized that music was a key to open doors to churches, colleges, and youth groups which would enable us to "tell it like it is."

Our writing careers seem to be doing well. We have already agreed to produce a book on the current changes in the Catholic Church for the publishing house, Stein and Day. Eventually, we hope to start our own publishing company, since we seem to be called to put more and more of our ideas into writing as well as music. A teaching-aid program which we have developed for use in parochial schools, called "Disco-Teach," is also in the workings. "Disco-Teach" provides realistic discussion material on the top tunes of the national charts and helps the teacher relate the world of the young people to ordinary classroom themes.

We were becoming deeply committed to many fields, but we all knew that one phase of our careers especially needed attention, and that was national television. Our story had been filmed by two major networks. Sunday feature sections of newspapers told our story across the countryside to huge audiences. We had been guests, also, on some of the "talk shows."

Friends told us we were a natural for the Ed Sullivan Show, and don't think we didn't try to get on! We met several times with his talent-coordinator who promised definitely he would put us on. He even waived the customary audition because he had seen us on a news show, and he liked what he saw. But . . . shortly thereafter, the talent-coordinator left the Sullivan show and we were left high and dry.

We met his replacement, Vince Calandra. We visited Vince at his office when we were in New York doing a series of concerts. We got along very well together and he promised to come to hear us perform that very night. After the show, we asked him, "What do you think?" He replied, "I think you guys are great. You're naturals for the Ed Sullivan Show."

Weeks passed, and no word. Months later, Father Berkery decided to call Ed Sullivan personally. His secretary answered, and intoned: "All acts have to go through the Sullivan office down at network headquarters, Father." What about my talking this over directly with Mr. Sullivan?" countered Father. "Not a chance," said the secretary. "You have to go through channels." Father crisply remarked to the secretary that it seemed easier to see the Pope than Ed Sullivan. That sparked the secretary and he asked Father where he was from. He soon filled in the blanks. "Seminarians? Work in the slums? Have a hot album?" Father's "yes" grew more enthusiastic each time.

"Why didn't you tell me in the first place?" They both laughed. "So you didn't get a date yet? Well, I'll speak to Mr. Sullivan myself. You know, he listened to the album and loved it. I'm surprised he hasn't contacted you yet. Give me until tomorrow. Okay, Father?"

The next morning, Ed Sullivan called to set a date for our group's appearance. It was to be on Easter Sunday.

"We may even have you on a few times after that," he added. "Keep up the good work."

We did the Sullivan show and, shortly after that, spots on several other national programs. We appeared several times on the Kraft Music Hall with Eddie Arnold and we got to know him quite well. We believe that he is really one of the warmest, kindest persons we have ever met. Anyone who does a show with him can be sure that Eddie will take a personal interest in him and, even more, will provide a very relaxing and easy-going atmosphere within which to work. Our lives are richer for having known him.

Eleven

Thanks to all the persons who have helped us, we have achieved a measure of success. Many have gone far out of their way to help us. If we are moving closer to the achievement of our goals, a large part of the credit must go to the great friends in the professional music world. They figuratively received us with open arms.

Once we were asked if we were out "to convert the wicked world of show business?" The question, of course, was tongue-in-cheek but there often has seemed to be a barrier between the world of religion and the world of show business. Organized religion seems to have waged a secret and undeclared war against show business.

Only recently have churches adopted a more liberal viewpoint toward shows and other entertainment. The discontinuance of such ratings groups as the Legion of Decency opens the way for greater rapport. Most serious members of the amusement industry have always tried to keep their programs above the level of "the world, the flesh, and the devil." But the industry, as with other groups, has sometimes been unjustly accused and stereotyped.

From our own experience, we have found the people we worked with were, as a rule, generous, gracious, and sincere. Their business, like any other, is to make money but they are also seriously interested in contributing to the general good. The people we associated with in the entertainment industry were extremely sensitive to anguish and quick to respond. They see a desperate need for responsibility and genuineness and they are eager to work with people in the church to offer positive, creative help.

We quickly found out that once we had entered the world of professional music, we could expect to stay there only on merits and ability. We had to be worth something; we had to produce. People will go an extra step for you when you wear a Roman collar. But, after that beginning, you must be able to deliver to stay in the running. Even before we embarked on our careers we knew this to be true. We never expected lasting favors because we were seminarians. We knew that for us to be effective we would have to be even better than the average new comer.

Normality was the characteristic that we strove for in our approach. But we demanded of ourselves excellence in our format and in our sound. And we worked hard for these. But any recording group just starting out needs some form of assistance and help. One cannot be expected to perfect his style and his total performance, and at the same time do a successful promotion job, deal with agents, and make the many necessary other contacts.

In our case, we were doing graduate work at the University, working in the slums, practicing, writing, and making many kinds of contacts. If we tried to carry on any additional promotional activity, we would have had to sacrifice somewhere; and perhaps that would mean giving up something more important in our long-range plan.

Even so, we found our agents could not really give us much help. They could not concentrate solely on us; they had many other clients. It was unrealistic for us to expect more from them. Although they constantly advised us against a personal manager, we had to follow our own ideas.

We had to do something. We were running into difficulty getting our albums distributed. They could not be found in the local stores. We were also told that we could make guest appearances on major talk shows, but that meant we would need a New York contact to represent us with the networks. Every kind of promotion costs time and money and both were scarce with us. So, we decided we *had* to get a personal manager to represent us and to counsel us on numerous details involved in launching a professional music career.

It's very easy to say: "Okay, let's get a personal manager." It's quite something else to find the right man. Whom do you choose, and why one man instead of another?

Our position was unique. We were a group "waiting to happen." We had many "plusses." We held a contract with a reputable recording company, we had a successful album, plus a proven concert program. Our sound was endorsed by many of the trade magazines and we had had national TV and radio exposure. Our single was getting good air play. Our newspaper publicity was excellent and nationwide. We had a definite date for the Ed Sullivan Show. And we had what we thought was one of the best musical directors in the country. Several people we approached were astounded at our promotional success; what we had accomplished by ourselves amazed even the most successful managers we visited.

It would look as if we could have signed any one as our manager. But really we wanted something more than an ordinary manager. Since our reason for becoming professional singers was unique, we were looking for someone who would understand our motives and our goals and, at the same time, one who could be a friend, advisor, and promotion man. We needed someone we could trust completely, who would somehow understand why we lived in the slums, and why we wanted to tell other people the stories we found in our work there. Our manager must be prepared to help us communicate what we felt must be told, for the good of the people we served.

After much careful and patient searching, we met such a man and he is now our personal manager. We considered him one of the best things that has happened to us. He is knowledgeable in the business and is respected throughout the country. We have worked with him for some time now, and we are greatly indebted to him and his staff for letting us benefit from their genius. There are few men whose abilities we respect more.

Our new manager is Gerard Purcell. He works with many well-known artists and musicians. We believe he agreed to take us on because he believes in us and appreciates what we are trying to accomplish. He is one person in the industry who feels that the Catholic Church should make some valid contributions to music in radio and television. He is well-known and well-equipped; he knows the right people. He has many friends not only because he is a warm person but because he always delivers what he promises.

With Gerry's direction, we were now able to move ahead. He is our spokesman; he "pushes" us; he "sells us." He studied our potential, put out modern, professional, promotional material on the work of The Mission, and blanketed the industry with our story and our message. He even re-negotiated our record contract. We believe our choice of a personal manager was a wise one, as each day proves.

He liked our sound, but he wanted us to "beef it up." When we appeared on the program of the Kraft Music Hall, the suggestion was made that perhaps we could use a little more "oomph." Some thought we sounded too soft, too gentle. Gerry felt that if we worked in the slums, if we were knee-deep in the nitty-gritty of everyday life, then our sound should come through as powerful, tough, gutsy.

Another problem appeared. Where do we go from here? Should we hire a few "ringers," professionals to sing with us? Should we play tapes in concert and just "lip-sinc" as many

other groups were doing? Should we increase our member-
ship? Gerry suggested perhaps we were not using all the
vocal power in the group, and that we should work first with
what we had. That meant more vocal coaching, more inten-
sive hours of practice.

Gerry was insistent that we work hard on our sound.
Suddenly we remembered Jack had been going to a vocal
coach for more than a year and he was very pleased with
what had been done for him alone. So John and Father
Berkery called to see if Jack's coach would be willing to
take on the whole group.

Jay Pielecki is a professional singer in his own right. He
uses the stage name of Jay Richards and has appeared on
local television frequently. When we met Jay, we found that
he knew quite a bit about us. He was sure he could help us;
what's more, he pinpointed our weaknesses and came up
with solutions for them. He agreed completely with Gerry
and knew just how we could "beef up" our sound. This he
said was simply a matter of applying some basic vocal
techniques.

Jay has a deep, rich, beautiful baritone voice. Yet he
has not concentrated on his own career. Rather he has chosen
to train voices, to work with youngsters through the public
school systems, and to give private lessons in voice development in his own home studios. He prefers what he is doing
now to anything else and all attempts to get him launched
on a professional career would be futile. He just is not
interested in it for himself. On an average week, Jay teaches
over one hundred and fifty students. There is no doubt that
Jay can sing better than the average person. We appreciate
his training, since we know that his voice is the product of
expert and highly specialized training received at some of
the finest vocal schools in New York.

Jay coaches us three times a week for more than three

hours at a time. On Saturdays he works with us all afternoon. He takes each of our songs and rehearses us to almost perfection. He says what we are trying to do is much too important for us to be satisfied with mediocrity. He has also taken one of the young boys we work with in the neighborhood and is training him, without a fee, to be lead singer with his group.

We know now we needed a coach. We could perform *much* better with little more effort under professional training. Jay made sure we received plenty of this latter. When we started to sing again in public, after working with Jay, people remarked how different we sounded, how much more impact we had vocally.

When Jay comes over to coach, we often get into heated discussions. After all, we feel we have been quite successful on our own. Jay is a typical music teacher—inexorable, sentimental, and deeply rooted in his own concepts of sound and rhythm. Working with a man of his temperament, hour after hour, week after week, tempers are bound to flame. Some of us were afraid at first that he would turn us into a different singing style. But our fears were unfounded. Jay never attempted to force his vocal interpretations on us. He only insisted that we be faultless in method, that we sing with feeling, and that we really *work* at our singing. He would stamp his feet, shake his head vigorously in opposition, but he always allowed our own personal style. We would go long into the night at times. He used sarcasm, silence, contempt just to pull us up. But once the session ended, he would sit and talk, and listen as we discussed our future plans and our present problems.

Jay is one of the great persons who have walked into our lives. He is part of us now. Not only did we get the best in vocal training when we got him, but we gained another close supporter.

We have the best manager possible and we also have an excellent, expert vocal coach. We seemed to be well on the way to our goal. But what would our own Church do to help us? Or, even, what would the authorities think about our national publicity?

At that time our provincial, who was also the head of our order in the United States, supported us publicly. Father Provincial travelled extensively, and he always boasted about "his boys." Once Father Berkery was asked if the provincial ever spoke about anything besides his St. Louis seminarians.

But the provincial seldom spoke to us individually. Whenever we met him, he'd paternally smile and say, "Make sure you don't neglect your studies, boys. Keep up the good work."

Father Provincial often discussed us with Father Berkery. As would be expected, some things about us he liked, others he did not. He did suggest that we try to get a professional record contract, so our records would get better distribution.

He allowed Father Berkery free reign in administering the seminary. He seldom interfered. He would say he didn't know much about on-campus situations and the problems involved, so he allowed the local superior to control his local situation.

Father Berkery is a prudent man so he was able to explain and support us. Father's vigilance and firmness kept any major problem from developing within his seminary community. But the nature of our own particular apostolate meant it would one day mushroom, and thereby consequences might develop which could not be foreseen.

Within our own archdiocese there was little official interest in us. Also, it was the policy of the officials of the University we attended not to interfere with individual religious groups; their concern was that proper scholastic standing be maintained and that other University requirements be met. There may have been those who did not completely approve of our work but they did not contact Father Berkery.

Many priests who worked directly with youth supported our work. They believed our efforts were worthwhile in religious communication. The Director of the Diocesan Youth Council invited us to produce the first folk-mass to be celebrated in St. Louis Cathedral.

The Church, in our area, did nothing either to help us or hurt us; they used our services when suitable.

The Mission is one sign of change within the Catholic Church, since Vatican II. Some values are different. We find the Church in the asphalt arena, with its battered and neglected homes that surround it. We find Christ in our brother.

Twelve

The following November a new provincial was named for our order who had spent twelve years as a foreign missionary. His concept of the Church was a conservative one and he considered part of his role to be a defender of sacred traditions. He seemed to consider renewal in the Church to be limited to simple outward signs such as turning the altar around so that the priest saying mass could face the people.

Our new provincial was not in complete sympathy with many of the changes that seemed to be taking place in the Church. To some extent his long time in active missionary life may have kept him out of touch with contemporary theological thought in this country.

After Pope John XXIII threw open the windows of the Catholic Church to modern currents of thought through Vatican II, many Catholics, both clergy and laity, seemed to divide between more traditional thinking and liberal thought. Our order was no exception in this respect, except that the appointment of a conservative provincial gave that group more influence. The liberals within our order were dismayed; some priests and senior seminarians talked openly of leaving the order.

Our seminary in St. Louis was nationally known, at least partly because of our singing group. The previous provincial had shown a free and liberal attitude. He himself was prudent enough to seek out competent counsel before making serious policy changes.

A few weeks after his appointment, the new provincial

made a visit to St. Louis. He stayed for several days at a near-by rectory and met with a group of priests, most of them conservatives, which did not include Father Berkery. There they planned the future of our order.

When the meetings were completed, the provincial moved quickly. He came, with another priest of our order, to see Father Berkery. He handed Father Berkery an official letter, stating that, effective immediately, he was removed from his position as superior of the seminary and appointed assistant pastor in a New York parish. The priest with the provincial was to be the new rector and superior. Father Berkery was directed to leave St. Louis that very afternoon.

As would be expected, Father Berkery was deeply hurt. He reminded the provincial that his actions were in violation of Church law, since a superior can be removed only after due process or after he has submitted a formal resignation to Rome. But the provincial was adamant. He had made up his mind that Father Berkery had to be transferred because he believed Father was hurting the seminary with his ideas.

We were all heartsick. We told Father Berkery that if he left, more than half the seminary would leave with him.

When Father Berkery saw the effect this decision of the provincial was having on us seminarians, he called the Superior General in Rome and explained what had happened. Father General was disturbed. He told Father Berkery to remain at his post as superior; he would come over from Rome to look into the situation and asked that the seminary keep operating.

The provincial had also called Rome and was told by the Superior General to delay any further action. He was told Father Berkery would remain as superior, and that the seminary should continue operating as it had been.

The provincial intended to follow the Superior General's directive. To act otherwise would have been an act of disobedience. However, his conservative advisors were anxious to see traditionalism triumph and so they prevailed upon him to keep to his original decision. He succumbed. He called a meeting of the entire seminary community, in direct contradiction of the Superior General, and he himself took over the administration of the seminary. At this meeting he directed that all inner-city stations be closed down; he forbade any continuance of work in the slums; he recalled all credit cards and car keys; and he announced that all seminary bank accounts had been frozen.

He did spend long hours with Father Berkery trying to effect some compromise. He could not understand why we seminarians objected to his actions.

When the provincial discovered that Father General was coming to the United States to look into the situation, he offered to resign. The provincial's conservative council would probably resign with him. But Father General knew that if that were to happen, it would be better for the welfare of the total order to lose one superior than to have an entire provincial administration walk out. He faced a dilemma. If he supported Father Berkery, he would need to go contrary to the duly appointed provincial.

Thirteen of us seminarians formally protested, according to Church Law, the actions of the provincial. We formally requested from Rome the special privilege of exclaustration. This was granted to us and we were thereby permitted legally to live outside of the seminary and away from the jurisdiction of the provincial until the situation was resolved.

The provincial also expressed his intentions of clipping our wings as a singing group. He called two of us to meet with him one night and read a dismissal edict, demanding that the two leave the seminary by the next day. He said he thought it would be better if they took time off to reconsider their religious commitment.

The cardinal who is head of the Sacred Congregation of Religious in Rome, at the request of the Superior General, sent a special representative to St. Louis to look into the problem. This special envoy decried many aspects of the situation, but in the end, he was powerless to remove the provincial. Father General still hoped some form of compromise could be reached which would make this unnecessary.

Father Berkery and John thereupon left for Rome to personally present our side of the issue to the Roman authorities. After the formal presentation of briefs of appeal and documentated evidence, Father General promised that he would personally conduct an investigation.

Throughout all this, we had not gone to the press or other news media. We had many close friends in the communications industry who would have wanted to report the controversy as news. Father General realized this and he had asked us not to take it to the press. We had agreed and we obeyed.

Father General gave Father Berkery a special leave of absence from the order, so that he could be with us, to help direct our activities and advise us. We moved out of the seminary, along with the other seminarians who had been recalled from their living quarters in Negro ghetto apartments by order of the provincial. We went back to our people, to continue what had been so suddenly interrupted. Our new group now numbers fourteen, including Father Berkery. All the seminarians are under exclaustration. We remained seminarians, and continued attending the University. We still planned to become priests; we were still members of our order. Although, according to Church Law, we were still within the order, and therefore had every right to its financial support, the provincial decided to deny us any money whatever from that source. We decided instead to go to work, at whatever jobs we could find, to obtain the money to pay our tuition at the University.

Many others worked against us. We found out that one of the conservative priests who had counseled Father Provincial, now sent a letter to the University, saying that we were no longer members of the order. Without support from our order, we were penniless; we had to get our lawyer to help us keep our guitars.

We were strictly on our own now but we had kept intact our ideals and our convictions. We had taken our stand. We were keenly disappointed that some of our "friends" had failed to support us. Although they were supposed to be champions of human right and dignity, they failed us in our real need. In the general confusion and dismay at the seminary, five younger seminarians asked to be dispensed from their vows.

We lived in the slums, continued at the University, and threw ourselves completely into our apostolate among the disadvantaged. After three months, the provincial suddenly released a story to the press that we had been dismissed from the seminary and that we were no longer studying to be priests. The news made the wire-services and national TV. We were labelled recalcitrants, rebels, heretics.

Despite the request of Father General to keep this problem out of the news, we felt forced to piece together our shattered reputations by telling our side of the story. Before it could be released, many people had phoned to call us vile names, labelling us hypocrites and phonies. On our rounds throughout the city, people even slammed doors in our faces.

It seemed as if our opponents were out to destroy our work. The week before our scheduled appearance on the Ed Sullivan show, the priest who had replaced Father Berkery as head of the seminary wrote to the producer that we should not be allowed on the show since we were not in good standing within our order. Every attempt was being made to discredit us and thereby cut off any means that we had of self-support, now that we had been denied funds from our order.

We felt we were really left no choice but to bring the whole situation out into the open. We had to explain our status, to show that we were actually studying for the priesthood, that we were not heretics, that although we were living outside the seminary, we were doing so with the full approval and proper authorization from Rome.

We released a statement to the press that we were awaiting the visit of the Superior General, who was coming to the United States in response to a legal appeal for juridical redress. The *St. Louis Post-Dispatch*, one of two metropolitan newspapers, took the time and trouble to find the facts of the story and to print our side of the controversy. The *St. Louis Review*, the diocesan paper, also did a story for us, one which the Archbishop of St. Louis praised as highly objective.

News magazines, religious newspapers, and local TV programs provided in-depth coverage for us. The wire services helped also.

Father General made his visit to the United States, as he had promised. But, all of a sudden it seemed, he refused to help us. He explained he felt he couldn't oppose existing authority. He asked instead that we forget what had happened, in the interest of peace. Someone reminded him there could be no peace without justice and Father General then agreed to come to speak with us.

We asked for a chance to appear before the assembled order to explain our situation. At first, this was agreed to, but later, approval was withdrawn.

Father General preferred not to meet with the lay

people who came in our behalf. He refused to see a Jesuit from the University who wanted to speak for us. He avoided all members of the press, radio, and television. His only concern was to effect some compromise, even if this meant our having to leave the order.

Father General told us he would hate to see our work and our apostolate lost to the order. But in the long run he told us he could not help us. We either had to obey the provincial or leave the order. We offered to agree to the former, if only we could be allowed to continue our work with the poor. But this permission could not be granted.

Father General suggested we might be sponsored as another group within the order, something within Church Law, but nonetheless offering us a chance to stay within our religious "family." He had done this for a French priest and his group only the month before. The provincial would not agree to this, however.

Father General left without notifying anyone. Father Berkery received a letter from him a few days later in which he promised to recommend our group to any bishop of our choice.

Although we seem to have been abandoned, we are still together, united in our common cause. We are fortunate in having found a group of priests who have since accepted us into their ranks. We still expect one day to be ordained as priests.

We can at least live with our consciences. We spoke up, took a stand, and remained completely within the requirements of Church law and order, with justice.

We have the "aura of legitimacy" about us once again. We have managed to weather a violent storm. But we have succeeded not by compromising ourselves and our basic beliefs. We did not sell out on our principles. We acted within our order as we have always acted on the streets and on the stage. We spoke out against injustice, cruelty, and the un-Christian abuse of power.

Since we were forced to leave our order, the order has suffered many other wounds. The pastor of a large parish in the East resigned after a sharp disagreement with the provincial. This priest had been an assistant to the previous provincial. He is now a secular priest. The provincial prefect of studies has also left the order and become a diocesan priest. Another superior resigned and entered the army. There are reports that other priests will be leaving. One member of the order for more than fifty years is now leaving for France.

We tell our side of this severance from the seminary of our order to preserve our good name so that we may continue to be useful to the people we serve. We hope, too, that more of the leaders of our Church will practice what is taught in recent encyclicals, such as Pope John's *Peace on Earth* and Pope Paul's *Development of Peoples,* and help all of us to reap the rich harvest of the renewal of Vatican II.

Thirteen

Now it is late August of 1969 and we are in Washington, performing for the National Liturgical Conference, which had been in session for three days before we arrived. We were surprised to see delegates dashing round, sporting huge colored buttons, saying, "Damn Everything but the Circus." The cardinal of the Washington Diocese refused to give his approval to the convention, stating that its professed theme of revolution was hardly relevant to liturgical rites and rituals. However, one thing seemed true; the conference was seriously trying to search out new forms of worship.

We had to drive more than five hours from New York to reach Washington and we arrived about six in the evening. The weather was extremely hot and humid. Our performance was scheduled for ten that same night. Omer Westendorf, President of the World Library of Sacred Music, met us in the lobby. He was the sponsor of the evening program and he was obviously relieved that we had finally arrived. Omer had recently commissioned The Mission to produce a long-playing album of twelve sacred songs. This we had done at studios in New York just before leaving for Washington, so we were able to give him the first copy of the album that night, even though it was only an acetate. He had invited us to Washington to introduce some key selections from the album, entitled *Soulful Sounds for a Church in Change*.

Downstairs where the program was to be held, we started to set up our equipment. Our instruments are almost entirely electrified now, and although it improves our sound, carting around the amplifiers is inconvenient and difficult.

Other groups were rehearsing when we walked in and our arrival with all our equipment only added to the confusion.

When we appear in concert, we ordinarily bring along our own drummer and organist as back-up musicians. We play the guitars ourselves, as also the bass and banjo. When we can't afford the travel for regular extra players we arrange to hire two musicians from the local union. In Washington, this meant more time consumed before we could begin to rehearse seriously. We had to go through each song several times right there on stage with the new musicians so they would be prepared for the actual concert. And time was at a premium.

Joe had written out lead sheets for both organist and drummer, along with a melody liner. But the drummer couldn't read music! That meant we had to teach him the parts right there on the spot; all this meant more delay and more trouble. We probably had been spoiled by the expertness of the recording studio musicians, who are top-grade; all they need is one run-through with a few written chords and they can improvise from that point. The drummer in Washington was not that skilled, so he required patient coaching. As it turned out, he proved skillful enough to cover his mistakes during the actual performance.

We always use union musicians because we ourselves are union members. We joined when we started to appear on national TV. It's a disturbing and little known fact that in St. Louis there are two locals, one for whites and the other for blacks. We joined the black union as a positive protest against such obvious discrimination. When we went to sign up, the head of the union local welcomed us in a pleasant manner but also told us that the white people had a union. When we expressed our intention to join his union, he was quite pleased. This local has been very kind to us. In fact, they have several times arranged special concerts for us.

Back in Washington we were on stage rehearsing our drummer right up to ten o'clock, almost to the minute the concert was scheduled to begin. We had no time to eat, but most of us were too preoccupied to remember that our last meal had been breakfast. As it turned out, it was nearly two in the morning before we were able to sit down to supper.

We were the first act on the program that night. The room swelled to a capacity of two thousand people. They were seated in the aisles, on the stairways, and on the floor. Chairs were not at a premium, they were gone.

The lights dimmed and on came a spotlight. We started our concert with a fast, upbeat song, *Freedom Rings* and followed with our theme song, *Yesterday's Gone*. The applause had barely died down when all of a sudden there was a commotion at the back of the auditorium. A group of priests, nuns, and seminarians entered the hall, clapping their hands and shouting, walking in single file. We figured it was to be a short demonstration, so we paused, we thought, briefly.

But the demonstation was not to be short or quiet. The shouts grew louder as the small group snaked its way down the center, screaming through cupped hands, "We protest Slovakia, we protest Slovakia."

The audience took up the rhythm, and the clapping become thunderous. Mob spirit began to take over and people left their seats in the audience to join the group. Soon the entire hall was encircled. The demonstrators stood on the outskirts of the audience, chanting, screaming and pointing, "We want you. We want you. We want you."

A voice announced that they wanted volunteers for a march on the Soviet Embassy. The chanting lasted more than twenty minutes; so we just stood back from the mikes and waited. Then we sat down, waiting for the display to end.

When they finally filed out of the auditorium, we resumed our concert to spontaneous applause. John cooly remarked that whenever the unexpected occurs, one should learn from Johnny Carson, who uses these untoward moments to bring on the commercials. So, John used the "break" to tell the audience about our latest album, *Soulful Sounds for a Church in Change.*

The demonstration at the Liturgical Conference brings up our own position on protest. In our age group, we are articulate champions of the dignity of man. But we feel strongly that the cause of freedom is not advanced by a disregard for the rights of others.

We have participated in numerous public rallies where protest was a major theme. We have given of our talents on many such occasions. But we insist that protest must be positive: this means getting involved, doing something. This does not mean we are against demonstrations. But we feel that action speaks louder than a mere parade. We try to live our concern as quietly and efficiently as possible. We think that if young people went into areas of need and rolled up their sleeves, they would unleash a powerful form of change which few could resist. Demonstrations serve a purpose, but unless backed by hard, positive action, they usually serve only to confuse and alienate.

What is tomorrow's direction for us? Where do we go from here? Before long, we hope to be priests. The kind of lives we lead now we consider to be an internship. It is real, with fulfillment accruing not in some distant tomorrow but also today.

Will we keep on singing after our ordination? We do not know yet. That's really not important. What is important is that we sing now, telling what we have seen and what we have heard. We continue to write new songs, even now preparing for more concerts and albums, digging in deeply in a field that we know shapes the destiny of man. We believe what one noted writer said: "Theology and philosophy of tomorrow are being developed in the performing and recording arts today." For these arts mirror faithfully the lives and frustrations, the dreams and hopes of men today.

We believe that man's first obligation is to spend his life fulfilling the promise of his personal creation, to literally make God's dream come true. In an age of exciting and yet sober developments, we of The Mission stand for human dignity, intelligent creativity, and responsible freedom. Our creed views the world as sacred, the Church as God-in-Man. To these beliefs we dedicate our lives and our actions. In these beliefs, is written our future.